INFINITE GROWTH MINDSET

DR GAJANAN SHIRKE

Made with ♥ on the Notion Press Platform
www.notionpress.com

This book is Dedicated to my daughters Rupeshi & Kavya and Rajeshree my lovely life partner for always loving and supporting me .

Contents

Preface

Being successful is a skill, It's meant to be hard, we grow by challenging ourselves mindset is required for growth. Infinite Growth Mindset is perfect book for professionals doubting themselves or struggling for growth. They'll discover how to nurture an awesome can-do attitude and celebrate mistakes and new opportunities as a path to success.

Acknowledgements

I would like to express a special debt of gratitude to my wife Rajeshree and my two daughters Rupeshi & Kavya. i also would like to thank every single person who every says " YOU HAVE TO READ THIS BOOK" , I just want people to remind each other how wonderful books are i dont care if its other book.

Enter Caption

About The Author

Gajanan Shirke, a hotel consultant, has years of extensive experience in the hospitality industry. His thirst for learning and aspiration to become a multi-faceted expert in the hotel industry helped him rise from employment to becoming an independent professional in the hospitality sector. Since his last assignment as General Manager at Kamat Hotels, he has become a renowned hotel consultant with a proven track record of developing, training and growing some of the best-known hotels, restaurants and fast-food joints in the Indian market. He was appointed as an expert consultant for The Eighth meeting of the Board of Studies for Hotel Management & Catering Technology. He is a visiting faculty at various Hotel Management Colleges and has trained over a thousand hospitality professionals. He has completed numerous pre and post opening hotel consultancies in India and overseas.

In order to spread his extensive knowledge to aspiring hotel professionals, Gajanan has penned a large number of books spanning different segments of the hospitality industry. Starting from his first book 'Bar Management and Operations' published in 2010, he has written 49 books including Hospitality Management, Food and Beverage Management, Hotel Engineering Management, Front Office Management, Hotel Housekeeping Management, The Cookery Trilogy: Advance Cookery Theory, The Cookery Trilogy: Foundation of Cookery, The Cookery Trilogy: The Basic Cookery Book, Hotel Sales and Marketing, Hospitality Industry Accounting & Fundamentals, Customer Interaction Excellence in Hospitality, History of Indian Cuisine – Volume 1, History of Indian Cuisine – Volume 2, Hotel Owner's Manual, Hotel Security & Prevention, Training Manager's Manual, Exceptional Service In Hospitality Six Sigma Way, etc.

Index

CHAPTER ONE

Failure is an opportunity to GROW

We all settle on success. We are excited when we succeed, and we love to hear or read about stories of success or of successful Leaders. But we usually forget that behind every story of success there are hundreds of instances of failure, stories of stumbling, falling and bouncing back. Happiness is only the epitome of a long process of pain, sadness, and frustration. Those who do it, those who understand the secret of success, have had to suffer through the toil of harsh defeat again and again, and sometimes in a state of solitude and total indifference. The world runs away from our failures, but celebrates with us on our successes. But failure only makes us if we accept it as part of life. Failure breaks only those who see it as total loss, as an end in itself. Failure is a wild horse you need to ride towards achievement and success. Successful individuals are experts in failure. Behind the happy face of achievement, lie stories of things broken, time lost, and wishes unachieved, and goals missed. The road to success is never embellished with beautiful flowers, soft carpets, or gorgeous sights! The savvy leaders are those who use the thousand failures as building blocks to rise higher. That is why they never get tired of trying, no matter how often they fail.

I always imagine success as this beautiful storyline, an epic of achievement, behind which a story of little and big failures are hidden, told and retold, to remind you of how far you have come, what steps you have taken before you learnt how to get it, how to do it. A child never gives up when trying to crawl, or stand up or walk- it takes him or her hours, days and months, filled with falls, cries and tears, before learning how to do it. A leader never gives up- he/she knows that pain will only abate when you reach the top of the mountain. The pain of giving up leaves more durable scars, than the pain of trying again and again and again. Successful leaders build on failure, live on failure and use failure to achieve, to succeed and to lead. The characteristics of those-who-fail-only-to-succeed are diverse.

Tips and advice as follows:

Do not be afraid to fail: Fear of failure is also a hidden fear of success Take big steps, jump higher, and dare to challenge conventional wisdom and common sense. If you don't risk anything, you won't gain anything. Everything you want is on the other side of fear." Mandela spent 27 years in jail, but refused to give up the struggle against apartheid, when presented with a fudged compromise. He was not afraid to say no and remain in jail, knowing that behind the indomitable image of fear and failure lies the bright picture of success.

Great success is built on great failures: Only those who dare to fail greatly can ever achieve greatly. If you want humans to get to Mars or Venus, you need to be prepared to get space missions to fail, shuttles to never reach destinations, technological devices to explode in the wide space, and obstacles to emerge by the hour, if not by the minute. Because your dream is big, so are your failures to achieve it. See your big failures as great lessons to learn from. Understand that the bigger you fail, the closer you get to your goal. Don't think limits, meaning that your dream to be a hero doesn't know limits, but only open vistas, limitless horizons. If you think limits, you create psychological hurdles to success. Dream big, fail big and enjoy huge successes all through.

Failure is the mother of inventiveness: Develop mindset says that you had not failed, but had found thousands ways what you had invented did not work. Experimenting and failing again and again is common to the great inventors who have changed our lives forever. Electricity in every home, thousands of planes buzzing in our skies on a daily basis, comfortable cars making far places within our reach in a few hours, smartphones making the world available to us through small screens that we gently tap with one finger, sophisticated machines that scan our bodies for malfunctions or illnesses, and a million other inventions- all of these would not have been possible if the inventors did not accept the rule that "if you don't fail and learn, you cannot succeed."

Failure is success suspendeduntil the moment is ripe: Sometimes we fail because we are ahead of our time, or because we are getting there but we need to think harder, work harder, and be more persistent. Remember Failure is delay, not defeat. It is a matter of finding the right solution for the right problem, and selling it to the right people, in the right conditions. The recipe to success takes special ingredients, and very minute and detailed dosage when it comes to seasoning. Failure can be essential to the solution itself, but it may be also a problem of packaging, marketing and communication. Therefore, failure is a matter of time- finding the right recipe to make the solution attractive and sellable in a timely fashion. Timing is key. Try again later but never give up.

You can know success only if you have experienced failure: The best perspective on success is through failure. It is failure that gives you the proper perspective on success. Success is built on held assumptions and found solutions. Some assumptions work and others don't. Therefore, every failed attempt gives you a sense of what doesn't work and what should work. Failure gives you perspective, it helps you focus and hone in on the right obstacles and the right solutions- things you could not have seen, had you not failed, had you not made assumptions that did not work.

It is okay to make mistakes: NOT okay not to learn from them Mistakes are the deficiencies that push us to aspire to perfection. In fact, they are not mistakes. They are our life lessons about what works and what does not work. That is why it is imperative to study our falls and our mistakes carefully to learn from them, to understand what could be key to success. The only real mistake is the one from which we learn nothing. Study carefully what does not work: therein lie the seeds that make you successful. The secret to achievement is made up of failures understood as warm-up exercises designed to help you learn to jump higher, aim better and get it right.

Success is a dream. But the road to success is surfaced with bold moves and brave acts. You have to risk something if you want to get something. In so doing, you are more vulnerable because you are exposed to danger, factoring in failure is a key characteristic of the bold leaders. Yes, they are afraid; but they know that overcoming fear can only happen when they espouse it and own it; if they fall, their fear does not grow; on the contrary, they become bolder, braver; they are vulnerable to bigger falls but also to greater achievements. Success is a thousand failures turned into a thousand lessons that allow you to overcome fear and catch the dream as it flies by you in a dark night. Don't be afraid to fail; be ready to succeed.

What happens then is that some of us take the loser label and define our future self-worth with it. We become reluctant to take risks. And yet, others become more determined to show everyone that they can be winners. No one likes the way failure makes us feel, but when we realize it's not the end of the road and we have time to come back as a success, failure can actually be a learning experience. What you can learn from failure can be invaluable to your future success. A close analysis of what went wrong with a failed idea or venture can help you make sense of the situation and learn lessons that will make you more successful the next time around. Being honest with yourself is the first step in turning failures into opportunities and learning experiences. Blaming failure on others or making excuses can only serve to dig you further into a state of denial. When that happens, you don't learn anything. If you don't use your failures to find flaws in your thinking, you're likely doomed to future failure. Being open to learning from past mistakes is a characteristic of every successful person. Remember, that every failure you experience shows that you tried. If you never fail at anything, chances are you are not trying hard enough to succeed.

CHAPTER TWO

You can learn to do anything

The best way to learn something new is to start doing something new. Don't put off your personal or professional projects when you can do them now.

Challenge yourself continuously and look for ways that can help you evolve your career. Gain expertise in what you want to master. Taking up difficult tasks can unleash your capabilities and help you discover your strengths and weaknesses.

Human beings do well at those tasks where they have a natural affinity or talent because that affinity enables them to progress at a relatively rapid rate, and so you get reinforcement which increases motivation and you continue to practice. There are people who definitely struggle when trying to learn something but for one reason or another, the desire to improve themselves is so strong, or the outcomes are so lucrative, or it just makes them feel good and they enjoy it, that they are willing to put in extraordinary amounts of effort.

We are born without skills, and we are able to learn everything that we need or want to learn.

Those who learn more effectively are the most curious and determined to acquire knowledge, and who accept their errors trying to improve by examining them (trial and error). If someone doesn't learn, usually it's because he doesn't want to, thinks that he lacks talent or is convinced of knowing already enough. You can find evidence in most biographies of successful people. Those who learnt something really well were often very bad at the beginning but had the determination to continue nevertheless.

When learning a new skill or lesson, changing the way you study it can help you master it faster. Reconsolidation a process in which existing memories are recalled and modified with new knowledge plays a key role in strengthening any skills. What I found is if you practice a slightly modified version of a task you want to master, you actually learn more and faster than if you just keep practicing the exact same thing multiple times in a row.

To be a master at something, you need to have some inherent capability but, even if you have talent, if you don't have the support and opportunity to develop that talent, then you are still likely to have difficulty in developing expertise. But it's not always the case that we learn things to be the world champion; we learn things because we get something out of it, whether it's the mastering of every small improvement we make, or a social aspect of just getting involved, or being part of a team, or fitness, or ultimately, just for the enjoyment of life.

Most of us often don't know how our brain learns, we tune out to learning. Knowing a little bit more about how your brain works can really help to be a little more compassionate with yourself when it might take you a little more time than another person to learn a topic. And, if it does take you a little more time, you might actually be able to learn it more deeply than the person who is a speedy learner. It's very valuable to learn more about how your brain operates, because then you can use it more effectively; it becomes a more effective tool.

Every good thing starts with a desire or eagerness to do something. The same goes for success stories. The more you keep pushing yourself to be knowledgeable and eager to learn, the clearer the way to success becomes. Curiosity not only helps you in excelling at the professional front, but a study found that it also improves memory and learning. The study revealed that curiosity releases a chemical linked with motivation, dopamine. Dopamine could motivate you more than any words ever could. Undoubtedly, without a genuine interest or curiosity to learn, you cannot expect yourself to be naturally inclined to learn new things. Eagerness to learn is where your success starts. Let's not forget that Newton discovered gravity when he was curious as to why the apple fell on the ground rather than going upwards. The list is endless.

Take up every learning opportunity that is presented to hone your skills. You can also continue taking informational interviews and job shadowing opportunities to keep your curiosity burning. Keep asking more questions and show that you are enthusiastic to learn. Also, reflect your curiosity towards learning by attending seminars, getting certifications, and enrolling yourself in online courses.

Try to be updated on current developments. Stay on top of the news as it can be feedstuff for all your conversations and could play a vital role in widening your network. Keep an eye on the latest trends in your field of work. You never know when something new will pop up and become the next big thing.

The attitude of learning is cultivated suppressing many temptations, avoiding short cuts and developing a fondness towards new experiences. There are few important things for living a successful and fulfilling life. You should never stop dreaming, never stop believing in yourself, never give up, never stop trying thus never stop learning. There are tremendous scopes of learning in every incident, you feel or you observe from a distance. The wisdom finds a learning lesson from every event of our life. Learn something from sadness, learn something from happiness, the setbacks should also give you a lesson learnt.

Teaching a skill enables you to understand it better too. Why? Because by teaching someone else, you first have to think critically about the skill or subject and break it down into easily explainable pieces. Ask a friend or coworker if you can discuss what you've been learning with them. Make an informative presentation about the subject or start a blog about your learning process.

- Say you're learning how to draw something, Craft a lesson plan! What techniques should they learn? In simplest terms, how would you explain working with pencil, or colours?
- However you decide to teach others about your chosen skill, practice explaining each concept with easy-to-follow steps. The better you can explain something, the better you understand it.

Learning to be eager to learn as an adult makes it easy for you to behave well in social situations. The constant drive to mastery is fuel to progress. It stimulates your creativity and helps you see the world from a different perspective. Knowledge gives you the ability to see connections you may have not noticed earlier. Your curiosity boosts your creativity, and your creative solutions will keep getting you curious to attain higher levels of perfection. That said, learning, unlike any other activity, requires active participation and trains your mind and body to perform at their fullest potential.

CHAPTER THREE

Challenges help you to grow

Challenges are a part of everyday life. They make us stronger and without them life becomes somewhat pointless because we have nothing to compare the good times to. These challenges come in many forms. For some, the challenge is doing well at work, for others it is getting to grips with financial worries. But, regardless of the challenge, facing up to it is key. Doing so will make you feel like you can take care of yourself, it will also make you understand the value of what you have now. It's truly fascinating how successful people approach problems. Where others see impenetrable barriers, they see challenges to embrace and obstacles to overcome.

Their confidence in the face of hardship is driven by the ability to let go of the negativity that holds so many otherwise sensible people back. Success isn't the only thing determined by your mindset. Optimists fare better; they treat failure as learning experiences and believe they can do better in the future. The first thing you must do is stop seeing challenges as problems, but start seeing them as opportunities. If you had a choice, you would probably seek to avoid challenges. However, despite your best effort to avoid them, challenges arise and threaten your journey; you must handle them.

In the muddiest times, you can blossom into the highest version. Thanks to those trials and tribulations, you gain the necessary wisdom and skills to be your best. By enduring and completing the process, you can teach others what you discovered. No matter how deep you are in the dark cave, keep crawling and inching forward. Regardless of how long and arduous the road may be, keep marching ahead. Even though you can't see it, there's light at the end of the tunnel. Keep trusting your heart and life's process. And in the dimmest nights, let your courage and determination shine through your day and give you the hope you need to persevere.

Challenges actually force you to tap into your creativity to come up with ways to overcome them. Some of the best ideas are conceived when you're feeling the pains of a challenge. Without the challenge, you would have never thought about that creative solution. When hurdles stand in your way, consider them as opportunities to find creative solutions to surmount them.

To build physical strength, you must apply a bit of resistance to your muscles. Challenges produce resistance, which develops inner fortitude. As you go through challenges, you become stronger and stronger. Challenges are an excellent opportunity for growth. They test your resolve and commitment to your goals. And when you overcome them, you develop emotional and mental strength.

Challenges remind us that we are human: we don't know everything; we can't foresee everything; we can't get away with everything; we have limitations; we have weaknesses; we make mistakes. Challenges remind us that we are fragile. The appropriate challenge can protect (or cure) us from becoming prideful.

By diversifying your skills and learning different processes, it can help you immensely when it comes to dealing with new challenges and change at the workplace. Think about what skills or knowledge you want to develop, and see if there's an opportunity that'll let you do just that. If possible, have a few concrete ideas in mind so you can suggest areas where you may be able to get more involved.

One of the key benefits of taking on new challenges is that you get to experience something that takes you to different horizons. When you're in a job for almost 3-4 years, you may have exhausted all learning opportunities and feel that you're ready to start the next chapter of your work life. In some instances, you've probably experienced symptoms of burnout or realise you're in a toxic work environment. Taking up a new job opportunity means you open yourself up to ongoing learning and making yourself available for further training and study options. When you're in a new position, you become aware of the many possibilities you can grow as a professional and you get exposed to different perspectives in both your work environment and colleagues.

Evaluate your day: This will give you a chance to look over your current responsibilities and assess what tasks you need to delegate to someone else or feel like it's not relevant anymore.

Analyse about what you want in your role: Are you looking to pursue a promotion at work? Analyse about the pathway you're currently on and consider challenging yourself in other ways that can help improve your professional life. Perhaps you can up skill with a short course or a nationally-recognised qualification. No matter what you decide, it's important to look at ways you can put your best foot forward at work.

Have an open and honest conversation: Being upfront with your boss about not feeling challenged can help improve your situation. If they have your best interests at heart, they will work together with you to come up with a plan on how they can delegate responsibilities that are not only challenging but ones that are equally full filling and engaging!

An organization's culture is embodied and maintained by its people. Take every opportunity to engage with your workforce, gauge people's views on how the company is performing, and give something back to those who have contributed to your achievements so far. With the cultural foundations that underpin your business intact, you can look to the future confident of achieving further growth and prosperity, whatever challenges arise.

When you have to overcome multiple challenges to reach your goal, you appreciate your achievement all the more; these challenges serve as amplifiers for your success. Certain accomplishments wouldn't feel as valuable if they were less challenging. When facing challenges, remember that they're opportunities that carry with them benefits: they call for your creativity, make you stronger, keep you humble, and amplify your achievements. Having the ability to put one foot in front of another despite not knowing what the outcome may be demands faithful courage. The bigger the fire, the stronger you'll be after overcoming it. Just like the lotus plant which blossoms into one of the most beautiful flowers in the world despite being in the dirtiest and murkiest environment found on planet Earth, he who conquers the most grueling and debilitating obstacles will evolve into his highest version. Embrace your masculine energy and make an empowering decision. Take a risk even if you are uncertain of the outcome. Fight for something you wholeheartedly believe in.

There are not many ways you get to test your leadership skills in a more challenging way than to be responsible for a major downsizing and complete it in a proper and respectful manner. This change of mind-set, which I saw as a unique leadership experience, made me place a high degree of focus, dedication and energy into making the process as fair and good as possible. The downsizing process was inevitable, so the problem was just as real, but by making a positive mental shift and focusing on the things I could still control, I dealt with the problem and process in a much better way, which strengthened me as a person and as a leader. Challenges and problems are important parts of life that give you experiences, make you learn and help you to become wiser and stronger. Problems make us grow and shape us. The biggest problem people have is that they hope for a life without problems. This is an impossible goal, and would lead to a boring life without character. We will all have problems – small or large – the difference is how we deal with the problems and challenges that occur. So don't run away from the problems and challenges you are facing in life. Don't ignore them or try to hide from them. Face them. Deal with them. The greatest growth in life and the most important lessons you will learn will come when you face and deal with a serious challenge or problem. Regardless of the result, value the experience and personal growth.

CHAPTER FOUR

Embrace Failure

Some individuals hold that a culture of success is one in which things must always run smoothly, with minimal or no mistakes. As such, they adopt a more divisive black-and-white approach to defining success and failure. This approach hinders your development. You become risk-averse, face anxiety and fear, and want to hide your mistakes, resulting in a stagnant culture with low team engagement and poor morale as well as high turnover and significant absenteeism. Be wise to accept and address failures at certain levels, learn from them, and move on without demoralizing and punishing teammates.

Today's successful individuals see failure as a teaching opportunity. It could involve mentoring new employees, holding debriefing sessions or providing training in a specific area where the failure occurred. Most important, failure should be explored and seen as an opportunity for everyone to learn and benefit. A culture that embraces failure promotes ongoing feedback, open communication channels and good listening skills. This way, employees feel able to approach their teammates before a minor mistake leads to a major disaster.

Empower people to make a call that will keep a guest coming back to the restaurant. Afterward, the leader and partner will recap what occurred with the guest and the decision the partner made. Review processes and use the 'mistake' as a teaching opportunity. Organizations that take a black-and-white approach to addressing failure leave no room for such experimentation. Unfortunately, this leads to risk-averse, non-collaborative behaviors that stymie opportunities for innovation and creativity. To stay relevant in our competitive economy, where ideas are invaluable, organizations must foster a culture of experimentation in which failure is acceptable—so long as the intentions are relevant and employees learn something from the experience. At a core level, organizations need to factor failure proactively by working it directly into their business plans. Organizations that neglect to see failures as opportunities for growth will ultimately find their failures ending poorly.

Taking risks and being willing to fail begins with our mindset. While some people seem to be wired this way, the willingness to take risks is a skill you can develop, whether you are an entrepreneur, executive or rising star.

Know your strengths and have proof points that illustrate those strengths based on the outcomes you've achieved. Taking a risk is easier when we come from a place of strength, knowledge and expertise. Where you have demonstrated good judgment and success is a great place to stretch because you are building on what you already know is true.

Debrief everything you do and be fearlessly open to giving and receiving feedback. Seeking root causes for failure will help you be more successful the next time because you learn what works and what doesn't. As you debrief, assess roles, responsibilities, structure, strategy and other areas where the project or idea went sideways. Feedback stings less over time when it becomes an opportunity for discovery and positive reinforcement rather than a source of pain and public embarrassment.

The shadow of the leader concept says that in organizations, people watch what others do and emulate that behavior over time. If you have children, you know that this is true. As a leader in your organization, decide what behavior you want to model, and observe how it translates in your team. If you model fear and suspicion, your team also will exhibit that behavior. If you truly support your team in taking risks and create a process to assess and honor risks and outcomes, your team will be much more willing to embrace the fear and move through it successfully.

Learning must become a deliberate practice and will require discipline. Just attending a random workshop or training session won't cut it. Being in conversation with others, testing ideas and thinking critically about what's important to you and your organization is a practice, not a drive-by behavior. I've had the benefit of working with and for several leaders who make a daily habit of journaling and setting aside time to think about their leadership and their industry. They also spend time in conversation with others as a way to build connections and foster learning about differing points of view.

Whenever you take a risk, you run into the chance of failure. Be willing to accept that. Even if you do fail, if you've taken the risk, you now know what works and what doesn't — and at the very least you've stretched yourself in a new direction.

Someone who has never had disagreements, and who has never experienced the difficulties that come with failure, doesn't really have the opportunity for growth. Failure builds character, and it shows you what you are made of. The way you embrace failure and deal with disappointment determines the way you achieve success, as well as how well you grow as a person. Great leaders have personal growth stories. They have been through difficult times, and they understand how to overcome adversity. Giving up at the first sign of trouble will never allow you to develop strength as a person, and it certainly won't provide you with the stamina to make it as an entrepreneur. Failure tests you and strengthens you and turns you into the person and the entrepreneur you want to be. While you don't want to intentionally fail at something, you do need to embrace the reality of failure. Don't dwell on your disappointments. Instead, learn from them, grow and move forward as a stronger entrepreneur with a stronger business.

We need to eliminate failure from our vocabulary when talking with coworkers and focus instead on how we might adjust our approach to reach our desired outcomes. Because failure is an essential part of the leadership model. Understanding that failing is a crucial part of the ideation process helps creative and entrepreneurs embrace their failure; internalizing lessons and constructive criticism that will help them shape their next iteration or attempt. The concept of "failing fast" allows innovators to rapidly cycle through several ideas with little regard for the ones that didn't work, facilitating experimentation, creativity and ultimately, progress.

Entry Level Professionals or students should be nicer to themselves — encountering failure is inevitable, but they have complete control over the mindset they choose to approach it with. Constant comparison with others in classes or online does nothing to boost self-esteem or self-confidence. At the end of the day, all one can do is be the best version of themselves that one can be, regardless of the grade one ends up with or the accolades one receives. Getting rejected once doesn't necessarily mean you should quit entirely and refocus your attention. It's simply a numbers game the more times that you put ourselves in unfamiliar and uncomfortable situations and experience rejection, the more unfazed you will be.

Remember Failures are Essential to Unlock the Door for Success: Failure is inevitable in life but it gives us the chance to jump back, to learn from our mistakes, and helps us to enjoy success. Failure can be disturbing, however success is all about going from failure to failure without losing enthusiasm.

1. Failure is the biggest and greatest Life's Teacher in everyone's life.
2. Failure will help you to reach new heights and reveal new potential for you.
3. Failure builds Character and makes you humble.
4. Failure builds and molds you into a strong person.

Ways to Grow From Failure

- Always be humble in every situation. Confession of your mistakes will make you relieve yourself and let go of your ego so that you can concentrate on your future ventures.
- Compassion. Acknowledging mistakes is upsetting, and almost unbearable but try to come out to start with a ray of hope and light.
- Openness to learning. Always believe in the learning process .We fail because lack of proper learning. Upskilling yourself is the biggest investment you can make for yourself.

Seek Feedback

It is your job to support and challenge your team, so that together, you can achieve the results you need. To do that effectively, however, you need to know if you are supporting and challenging your teammates in the right ways or if, despite your good intentions, you are holding them back. You need to know what you do well, so you can build on it, and you need to understand your weaknesses, so you can correct them. In short, you need feedback.

Always ask some of your contacts within the company for their insights. If you are really brave, you can even ask what they hear about you. A helpful starting point is to ask your own supervisor about his or her observations of your management style. You can also ask your colleagues who are also managers about their own styles, which can open the door to a discussion about the way you manage your team and any feedback they may have for you.

Do you have a trusted friend or mentor in the company? Let him/her know your interest in strengthening your leadership style, and ask if she has heard feedback that s/he would be willing to share (without disclosing the sources, of course).

Effective feedback, both positive and negative, is very helpful. Feedback is treasured information that will be used to make important decisions. Top performing companies are top performing companies because they consistently search for ways to make their best even better. For top performing companies continuous improvement is not just a showy slogan. It's a true focus based on feedback from across the entire organization customers, clients, employees, suppliers, vendors, and stakeholders. Top performing companies are not only good at accepting feedback, they deliberately ask for feedback. And they know that feedback is helpful only when it highlights weaknesses as well as strengths. Effective feedback has benefits for the giver, the receiver, and the wider organization. Here are five reasons why feedback is so important

Our unconscious brain knows something that our conscious brain often forgets: confident people generally perform better than insecure people. When we think we have a good chance at succeeding, we tend to try harder and persist longer. Because confidence is key to survival, we have developed several security mechanisms to protect our fragile egos. One of these security mechanisms is called the Self-Enhancement Bias. Our brain tricks us into believing that other people's successes are the result of good luck and their failures are well deserved, whereas our failures are a result of bad luck and our successes are well earned. While the self-enhancement bias effectively bolsters our confidence and does motivate us to achieve, if left unchecked, over-inflated egos create unhealthy self-delusion that can result in narcissism, selfishness, broken relationships and poorer outcomes—if not for the individual, then certainly for those who are impacted by their behavior. Feedback is the reality check we need to calibrate our confidence to ensure it continues to work for us, instead of spilling into overconfidence, which works against us.

Ask someone in your organization when feedback occurs, they will typically mention an employee survey, performance appraisal, or training evaluation. In actuality, feedback is around us all the time. Every time we speak to a person, employee, customer, vendor, etc., we communicate feedback. In actuality, it is impossible not to give feedback. Feedback can actually motivate employees to perform better. Employees like to feel valued and appreciate being asked to provide feedback that can help formulate business decisions. And feedback from client, suppliers, vendors, and stakeholders can be used to motivate to build better working relations. Invest time in asking and learning about how others experience working with your organization. Continued feedback is important across the entire organization in order to remain aligned to goals, create strategies, develop products and services improvements, improve relationships, and much more. Continued learning is the key to improving.

Feedback is one of the most powerful influences on performance. We do better when we have an accurate understanding of how closely our current performance stands in relation to our desired performance. Sprinters need feedback from the stopwatch to know if their new training regimen is working. We lose weight more effectively if we weigh ourselves every day. My presentations get better when clients tell me what they felt went well and what they would suggest I do differently next time. Reaffirming feedback tells us that we are on target and encourages us to continue to do what's working. Helpful feedback, as I refer to it, gives us ideas on how we can improve. Research, and common sense, leave no doubt that feedback greatly improves performance.

The bottommost line is that people in leadership positions, including all levels of management, must become experts at requesting feedback it they want to become a more effective leader.

CHAPTER SIX

I am inspire by the success of others

There are many characteristics that have the power to inspire and uplift you. You can learn how to get inspired by leaders success their courage, drive, creativity, or passion for life.

These are some of the many qualities of an inspirational Individuals:

- Believes in themselves and has self-confidence
- Stands up for their personal values
- Doesn't shy away from challenges
- Speaks up for themselves
- Handles difficult situations with compassion
- Is fair
- Admits fault and takes responsibility
- Refuses to accept unjust behavior
- Communicates clearly and follows up words with actions
- Aims to make a difference

Look to the people who are doing what you want to do and ask them for counsel and advice. Which hotel in Nagpur was best? Where did you buy that engagement ring? What platform do you use for your blog? Can you take a look at my business plan? These, and countless other questions, are things you can run by experienced peers. Get all of the free advice you can because the people you are asking will likely be more than happy to help. These people understand the value of exchanging ideas, working together and collaborating. Use their wisdom to ensure you don't make the same mistakes as those who came before you.

We all wish success could be transmissible, like the common cold make out with a billionaire and wake up a tycoon. Sadly, this is not how it works; but, spending time with happy and successful people can inspire you to reach your potential. It is about seizing opportunity, being resourceful, adapting and making the most of any and all situations in which you may find yourself. You really are the product of those with whom you associate. We may suffer from misunderstandings of grandeur, but really, if your friends are not living up to their potentials and challenging themselves, you likely aren't either.

By spending time with and learning from driven, ambitious and successful people, you will start to familiarize and, in turn, adopt their mentality. Put yourself in situations that hold the promise of adventure and opportunity. This will allow you, in a sense, to absorb the successful traits of those around you so that you can incorporate them into your lifestyle.

Do not compare your life to anyone else's because you will never know the whole story. This will only lead you to second-guess every decision you make and further delay your eventual success and growth. Separate yourself from the negativity because it will do nothing but bring you down. Examine other people's successes with hope, not jealousy. Allow their successes to ignite your perseverance and determination. When you're true to yourself, your life will be better.

Sometimes your circumstances are beyond your control, and for whatever reason, you may find yourself in difficult or challenging situations. If you don't understand your full potential, it is easy for these situations to bring your down. When we refer stories where others were able to overcome their circumstances, we are learning ways out of our own. Success stories help us understand that our circumstances don't define who we are. How we react to them does. A lot of life is entirely in our control when we look outside of the environments we may find ourselves in. Opening up his own perspective and listening to others. It's about learning from each other and knowing you have similar people in your corner.

If someone has been successful, you can learn from their story and incorporate their approach into your own life. All of these stories can create a roadmap for those embarking on their journeys towards success. Success stories bring awareness to the truth in our lives while emphasizing that life is indeed beautiful.

Leaders who inspire us to be better are not weak, scared or stuck. They are bold and have the determination and courage to push through their fears, and take a stand on what they believe. They have done what we call brave up. They have developed the bravery required to become positive, strong, and influential in the world today. These inspirers have faced great odds and challenges, and they have turned their clutter into a message to help others overcome their challenges too. They are warriors, and brave fighters for what they believe in and how they see themselves and the world. They have figured out that if you want to make a difference in the world, you have to address your own demons first. They no longer worry that they will be rejected, scorned and put down. They have grown beyond feeling they have to hide or suppress parts of themselves to be accepted.

CHAPTER SEVEN

I like to try new things

If starting something new doesn't come easily for you, you are not alone. We have met senior leaders who were hesitant to speak up for the first time or take a chance on something new when they'd had success with the tried and true. Learning something new helps build new brain cells and can strengthen connections between the cells. Accessing new information can come from a variety of sources including podcasts, books, video channels, and your own personal connections. To help you implement this practice into your daily life, we tapped several experts about the benefits of learning something new every day, and how to make the process easier. Working to feed your mind a new tidbit of information regularly will keep the organ sharp and alert. Beyond benefiting your brain, unlocking new information also fulfills a human need as well. Humans crave novelty and growth. Learning something new daily allows you to meet those needs.

My precise attention to professional development, mentoring, and succession planning have shown me that being focused on the end result is much more important than how you get there. Many companies, organizations, and businesses have established detailed programs to prepare their future leaders for the opportunities that may present themselves. There is great value and security in ensuring that the three principle elements of professional development: education, training, and experience have been included in a leader's growth environment and formative years. One of the leadership negatives that accompany highly structured and deliberate growth programs is the loss of desire/ability to try new things. This can lead to trouble in a dynamic environment where leader agility, speed of action, and ability to experiment with new ideas is critical to mission success, adaptability, and organizational longevity.

Trying new things is paramount to being a successful person, building a complete human one that you will be proud of. So, when was the last time you did something for the first time? Coordination is okay. After all, nobody wants to be a mess. But there is fun in messiness. Sometimes, it pays to scatter just to see if you are capable of fixing it back together. Life and longevity are two gifts we can control how well we use them. Believe it or not, the more new and fun things you do, the more fulfilling and satisfying your life becomes. People who seek out new terrains and activities are happier, positive, alive, and healthier. Step out of your comfortable box and introduce something new every day. The standard is monotonous and outdated. If you are not the type of person open to drastic changes in your life, take it one step at a time. Nobody is forcing you to eat something you don't like to eat. You can start with progressive comfort food. Stop giving yourself excuses to remain mediocre in your life. It is time to stop empowering factors that limit you (or so you thought) from experiencing something new in your life.

New things slow you down enough to make you appreciate your surroundings and move you away from boring routines. As we grow older, the days and minutes seem to pass away without any noticeable event happening around us. We suddenly find ourselves with nothing interesting until the holidays or when something new happens in the family. For some of us, it is never because we live in isolation. However, when you try new things, you slow down time and appreciate the time you have in your hands. Keep your hand busy with something new outside work and the regular clique. If you are adventurous enough, you will come back with new life lessons, friends, and perspectives. Overall, you will become a well-rounded person

Try new things today and open yourself to new emotions, experiences, and cultures. It is boring recycling the same old things over and over again. Whether it is a new haircut, food, hobby, or experience, there is fun in adding a new thing to your life portfolio. It is humbling to break away from your routine and tick something off of the bucket list. Life is too short to remain in one place without any stories or memories of new things you did on your own. So, this is the time to try new things—from simple tasks to daring and challenging ones, add some spice to your life. Remember that fear is a drawback, so conquer it by pushing yourself out of your comfort zone. When you learn something new every day, you and everyone around you benefit from your new knowledge. And, unlike when you were at school, you can choose to only learn the things that interest you. There are unlimited ways to do this, and we've only touched upon several of them.

If you find it difficult to retain new information, take some time to figure out what learning style works best for you. Some people are visual learners, while others are audible. Some people enjoy reading while others, like myself, learn best from experience. To determine your preferred way of learning, try a few different methods and see which one keeps you engaged for the longest period of time without getting distracted. If you're trying to expand your knowledge on something particularly challenging, searching online for the best way to learn that specific subject. Alternatively, asking friends and family members what has helped them learn new things in the past or to think about techniques that worked for you in prior times and replicate those methods

Sample List of something new to do/try everyday

- **Meet someone new.** Talk to a stranger, learn about them, and try to make a friend.
- **Try a new skill.** Whether it's a musical instrument or a sport, just try out something you would normally never do; the more outrageous it is the better.
- **Find a new way to get everything done.** Instead of doing the same thing you do every day, try a new way to get it done. A new way to work, a new way to do your work, or a new way to cook a certain meal.
- **Try different times to fall asleep and get up.** There is a different time that works best for everyone, and ours may only differ by a few minutes, trying different times can result in the perfect amount of sleep every day.
- **Test how many, and how long, your breaks should be.** One day try out taking hour breaks, the next try taking 45 second breaks, see what works best in what situations. Everything that saves time increases productivity, which leads to success faster.
- **Get out of your comfort zone.** Do something that makes you feel uncomfortable and beat it, every single day.

CHAPTER EIGHT

Challenge yourself often never settle in life

Life is an uncertain roller coaster. You can choose to embrace it and enjoy the ride, joyfully learning from your experiences along the way; or you can choose to rebel against all of life's challenges, resenting every moment of your journey. You have to set new goals for yourself, and you are ready to work hard to achieve them. A challenge is something that teaches you how to grow as a person. They encourage personal development and are a way to work on self-improvement. They aren't supposed to be easy and accomplished without any effort. Challenging things to do might look different for you than it does for your coworkers, siblings, or friends, but that's OK. Your challenges could seem like little things, like trying to wake up earlier or shake bad habits like smoking, but they are still challenges. Everyone's experience is different. In fact, that's the beauty of a challenge. It opens you up to new experiences and puts in the effort to improve yourself every day. It lets you really focus on yourself. Whether you are challenging yourself to de clutter and stay organized or run a marathon, the challenges you set for yourself to overcome are entirely your own.

When you challenge yourself, you push your boundaries and grow as an individual. When you rode a bike for the first time, you were probably scared that you would fall and hurt yourself, but with a little help you started pedaling and at the blink of an eye, you were riding a bike – you had learned a new skill! As kids, we grow as individuals almost every day – why stop when we grow older? When you challenge yourself, you push yourself to fully realize your potential; and I am sure your potential is greater than you might think. Stepping out of your comfort zone is scary. Actually, it can be downright terrifying. Whether it's being asked to do something high level at work or trying to do a new yoga pose, challenges are meant to scare you. Use that fear and the adrenaline in your favor.

You should challenge yourself to discover more about who you are, what you like, what you do not like, and what you are passionate about. As you succeed in the challenges you give yourself, you will find confidence in who you are and your abilities and confidence, I have found so far, is a crucial characteristic to finding the path to success, no matter what success is to you. If you do not believe in yourself, how can you expect others to believe in you? Therefore, it is so important to consistently challenge yourself to constantly build confidence and a great self-esteem. You will never be able to build self-esteem from others approval; only by finding confidence in who you are as you overcome the inevitable challenges of life and the challenges you give yourself to realize your full potential. Remember the story about kids riding their bikes? Why do you think they are smiling all over their faces? Because they just overcame a challenge, realized a greater amount of their potential, and gained confidence in themselves. Not from others approval, but their own confidence in their abilities.

If you want to start challenging yourself even more in your daily life, you can take the first step and start with a small challenge. It can be all from doing 20 pushups every day the important thing is just that you take the first step towards more challenges. Because when you succeed in the first small challenge you give yourself, you will be filled with confidence and courage to take on a new, slightly bigger challenge which will result in more personal growth, greater self-esteem, and new passions – who knows, you might end up learning New Language at some point.

When you have given yourself a small challenge that is realistic and concrete, it is important that you engage in consistent action. Therefore, it is essential that you do something every day that takes you just a tiny bit closer to achieving your goal. Now, it does not have to be a huge part of your day, every day. For instance, you could keep a diary of you daily progress or write down in the morning what you aim to achieve throughout the day, so you commit to achieving your goal every day. If you want to achieve your goal, you must work on it consistently. So we would commit to progressing every single day – because that is how you succeed in your challenges.

New challenges aren't something that everyone will look at and feel like jumping into right away. But that's part of the challenge itself. As you learn that personal growth starts outside of your comfort zone, you'll be more inclined to learn how to challenge yourself. The positive thing is that you don't have to do all of these self-improvement challenges simultaneously.

Pace yourself, and be proud of your accomplishments.

CHAPTER NINE

A pure growth mindset

It enables intelligence to mature, embraces challenges, is resilient and grows in tandem with inspiration from a liked-minded community. The opposite is a fixed mindset, where people believe the opposite of the growth mindset - that intelligence is fixed and cannot be grown. In preparing an ecosystem for change, developing a growth mindset is critical to confronting the challenges of a new learning pattern. Given that the challenge is to unite a global learning community, growth mindsets are needed to support the processes involving ideation, prototyping and evaluating. If educators wish to create a paradigm shift, there must be a high level of agility, flexibility and 'failing-forward' to deal with continued change. Parents, likewise, must develop a growth mindset. Their knowledge of and commitment to growth mindsets will benefit the new paradigm, their children and themselves.

Most of us often confuse a growth mindset with being flexible or open minded or with having a positive outlook qualities they believe they have simply always had. Everyone is actually a mixture of fixed and growth mindsets, and that mixture continually evolves with experience. A pure growth mindset doesn't exist, which we have to acknowledge in order to attain the benefits we pursue. Unproductive effort is never a good thing. It is critical to reward not just effort but learning and progress, and to emphasize the processes that yield these things, such as seeking help from others, trying new strategies, and capitalizing on setbacks to move forward effectively. In all of our research, the outcome the bottom line follows from deeply engaging in these processes.

A growth mindset can help you become more resilient in the face of setbacks. When you come across a difficult situation, you're more likely to frame it as a challenge to be overcome rather than a reason to throw in the towel. You become better able to persist in the face of adversity and achieve your goals.

A growth mindset can help you become more adaptable. Rather than feeling overwhelmed or threatened by big changes, you are more likely to see them as opportunities to learn, grow, and reinvent yourself. You can embrace new challenges and use them to your advantage.

A growth mindset can help you cultivate a positive attitude. When you believe that your capacity to improve your own talents is unlimited, failure stops being something to be frightened of. You can approach challenges with optimism and confidence, which makes you a better leader and fosters a more positive work environment.

Change doesn't happen overnight, but if you can build small, positive actions into your daily routine such as meditating after you brush your teeth you can turn them into habits. Take on a project doing something you have no experience with. Try a new hobby, play a new sport, or challenge yourself to do something you have never done before, such as speaking in front of an audience.

It takes time to develop a growth mindset, so don't be dismayed if you don't see results. Instead, focus on consistency. Take positive steps each day and trust that the results will come in time. Books are an invaluable source of new ideas and viewpoints, and can expose you to novel ways of seeing the world that you hadn't considered before. Exploring new subject matter with an open mind can also help you view existing challenges in a new light, making it easier to spot solutions you might otherwise have missed.

Praise the effort of your teams granted, if someone spent a week on a task that should have taken a few hours, it is not helpful to reward the unnecessary effort. What we mean by this is, when a goal is successfully met, it is critical to reward the learning and progress and to emphasise the processes that yield the goal, such as seeking help from others and trying new strategies, rather than simply acknowledging and rewarding the goal itself. Similarly, when a goal hasn't been met, but successful effort and changes have been made in approach, this should also be praised. The outcome may have been outside of the individual's control. By praising effort and progress in approach, the individual will continue to persevere and apply learnings in future scenarios, enabling them to reach successful outcomes.

Do not let yourself be threatened by others you perceive to be better than you, identify what you can learn from them one scenario that has us quickly defaulting back to our Fixed Mindsets is the perceived threat of someone who is better than us. As the saying goes 'comparison is the thief of joy' and it is also the thief of the opportunity to develop. Rather than being threatened by others who you perceive to be better than you, identify the skills they have that you don't possess yet and think about how you can learn from them.

Make growth mindsets part of the mission statement. Leaders must deliberately include growth mindsets for learning in their mission. The mission should be visible and regularly discussed to encourage its implementation.

Enable community and professional development. Opportunities of developing a growth mindset should be available for all key actors in the learning community, including parents and guardians.

Insist on effective communication. Parents are critical influencers on a learning community and leadership must create a culture of strong communication to be in regular contact with them to ensure support exists for all learners.

Create growth mindset learning experiences. Learning experiences must be active, reflective and foster the skills that learners require to succeed in the 21st century. Learners must learn how to learn, learn about growth mindsets, grit, brain plasticity and anything else in support of personal growth.

Ensure collaborative learning is present. Learning guides should facilitate learning experiences that communicates a culture of collaborative support.

Ensure risk is present and embraced. The learning community should praise risk even if failure is the result. This dissolves taboos that failure in learning is negative. A culture of risk encourages learners to take on challenges that stretch their skills.

Become comfortable with failure – if you feel like everything you do has to be a success, you may be stifling innovation and creativity by not trying new things or taking risks. Know that the worse that can happen if you fail is that you're going to discover that you're human and you're learning just like everybody else. Find ways to make failure and struggle the norm, be prepared for multiple attempts to get the result you're looking for, share your struggles with others, and seek help or mentoring when you need it.

Practice self-compassion – no matter how much you embrace a growth mindset, and believe that your talents can be developed, certain situations and people may still trigger your fixed mindset. It might be when you've made a mistake, especially if it's a public mistake, or you've been criticized, or are starting a new job. In these moments you can feel hurt, humiliated or overwhelmed, and your self-critical voices can be telling you that you don't have real talent or that your reputation is at stake. Carol advises to become aware of your triggers, and when these arise show yourself some self-compassion by acknowledging the critical fixed mindset voice inside your head that's undermining you. While it may be just trying to protect you, gently remind yourself that you are trying to develop a more growth mindset, and making mistakes is just part of this. Ask your inner self-critic to support you to take on new challenges and learn new things.

Go after grandiose ambitious goals, with the understanding that while some are going to hit the moon and catapult your organization into the future, others may not, but still can provide valuable learning and development opportunities. For employees to continuously develop a growth mindset, leaders have to promote it with encouragement, praise, and recognition for their efforts. This does not mean that leaders should excuse, overlook, or ignore poor performance. The goal is to provide an environment that helps employees see their role in exploring new possibilities.

Developing a growth mindset relies on various areas of an individual's life, often beyond their control, being appropriately aligned to support them, specifically the learning community, educators and parents. This section sets out to formulate how to prepare and implement these key areas to create the optimum conditions that support the fostering of growth mindsets.

CHAPTER TEN

Growth mindset, kaizen leaders

The motive to be better than you were yesterday. By continually improving every aspect of our lives - be it professional or personal, we can strive forward & be the best versions of ourselves that we always aspire to be.

'Kaizen' is the Japanese word (Kai = change/improvement, Zen = good) about achieving improvements by taking small steps instead of radical/drastic changes. These small increments lead to significant improvements over time, which is why Kaizen has been the go-to method for process improvement.

The Kaizen philosophy is based on ten principles:

1. Let go of assumptions
2. Be proactive
3. Challenge the status quo
4. Let go of perfectionism & take an approach of iterative, adaptive change
5. Look for answers
6. Create a surrounding in which everyone feels empowered to contribute
7. Do not accept the apparent issue; instead, ask "why" several times to get to the root cause
8. Involve several people in the process & ask for their opinions
9. Use creativity to find low-cost, small improvements
10. Never stop improving

If you have a fixed mindset, you believe that your potential & character are unalterable & have been written in stone since birth. You assume that they can't be improved or modified in a meaningful way. Thus, any success in this kind of mindset results from inherited talent, the given resources,

& the environment you were born in. Instead of thinking of improving yourself, you hope that other people will be less competent than you. Furthermore, it leads to a desire only to look smarter, but not improve yourself. The result of the fixed mindset is that people don't develop their intellectual competencies over time. The other option is having a growth mindset. It means that you believe in improving your character & personal evolution by working on yourself. You see yourself as being at a particular starting point with the option to experiment, test new ideas, & improve yourself continually your skill, beliefs, & competencies. In the growth mindset, intelligence isn't stagnant, but rather one that can be developed. Instead of looking smart, it leads you to build intelligence by continually learning, thus improving yourself overall. Another positive result is the mindset of embracing challenges, seeing effort as the path to mastery, being inspired by others' success &, learning from criticism. You see everything as a skill, & every skill can be practiced & improved. With a growth mindset, flaws & problems are only opportunities to improve. Unknown & new things bring learning opportunities, mastery leads to passion & purpose, & every failure is only a temporary setback. Therefore, the growth mindset leads to tremendous personal success, self-esteem & self-confidence, constant learning, better relationships, avoiding perfectionism, & becoming the best version of yourself.

A growth mindset is an essential requirement for cultivating the Kaizen culture. We might say that Kaizen's spirit is more about finding the flow of change rather than looking for measurable steps. This isn't to say that massive improvements do not occur. However, the point is that you are not striving for brilliant insights but merely trying to do a little better moment by moment. In essence, aim for micro improvements in your day-to-day life. Do not overthink it; get going with it. What you will find as time passes are subtle continual improvements that will empower you to set the next set of goals. Those with a **growth mindset** believe that success is directly related to constant learning and the effort you make and that the results of any experiment are not meant to prove whether or not you are smart. These are people who recognize their mistakes and learn from them. In fact, they are thrilled to continue learning when something goes wrong. Their confidence doesn't stem from their intelligence but from their dedication. They have the power to overcome problems and improve.

Here are a few ideas on how to start implementing Kaizen:

- **Organize a Kaizen event** with your employees and brainstorm as many ideas as possible on how to improve your organization.
- **Select the most obvious problem in your organization** and try to solve it with using the PDCA cycle (Plan-Do-Check-Act).
- **Start by analyzing where your organization produces the most waste,** either in materials, in the production process, or in the daily use of employees' time
- **Introduce the Zenkai quarterly title** for a person who makes the greatest contribution to the improvement of your organization.
- **Start a coaching program in your organization,** so that employees can develop the growth mentality more quickly and start helping to shape the Kaizen culture.

While there are many resources available to guide you through your kaizen efforts, it's important to personally understand your kaizen journey. Reflecting on your kaizen efforts after improvements have been implemented is an important part of the continuous improvement cycle. As you reflect on your efforts, develop your own kaizen guidelines. Start by creating guidelines based on your own experiences improving the workplace. Keep in mind that these guidelines should be for your colleagues, your successors, and yourself to understand the problems you have overcome. These guidelines will ultimately help you as you approach your next challenge. The process of implementing Kaizen requires a long-term commitment to a series of efforts and improvements. Building a mindset of continuous improvement among your culture requires daily practice, and with time, you'll see an increase in the efficiency, productivity, and quality of your operations.

CHAPTER ELEVEN

Six Sigma methodologies to grow

Six Sigma is a method that offers tools to improve your capabilities in managing your businesses. This increase in performance and decreasing process variation, it is possible to reduce defect rates, improve employee morale, and improve the quality of products or services, which all contribute to a higher level of profitability. Six Sigma can be applied to any process in any industry to establish a management system for identifying errors and eliminating them. It provides methods to improve the efficiency of business structure and quality of processes, enhancing the profitability of the business.

Tools Used For Quality Improvement

- DMAIC [Define-Measure-Analyze-Improve-Control]: Using this data-driven template to improve current processes is an essential part of this strategy.
- 5s: This tool stands for Sort, Straighten, Shine, Standardize, and Sustain. This is a great way to simplify and streamline your workplace or area. This is used to eliminate waste on the most basic level.
- 7 Wastes: These are non-value added losses and include Inventory, Motion, Over processing, Overproduction, Waiting, Transport, and Defects.
- Value Stream Mapping: This could be the most important of the Lean Six Sigma tools and techniques because it allows you to visually see the entire process from start to finish. This includes a drawing of a future state map and of how value should be flowing once changes are implemented.
- Flow: This is shown in that future state map from design to launch.

You are planning to launch a new product. From creating the hype to announcing the launch event date and everything in between, you have done everything to make the product launch a success. Your product launch event made the headlines and received a great response from the audience. As the marketing hype starts to settle after a few weeks, you start to receive customer complaints about defects in products. Whether it is through your social media pages, review sites or emails in your inbox, your brand is earning a bad reputation. Finally, you will have to discontinue the product and recall the remaining stock from stores. This would not have happened if you have implemented lean six sigma or paid attention to improving the quality of the product.

Lean Six Sigma is a methodology used to minimize defects and errors and improve the process. It is one of the most powerful frameworks to develop better products and services. Six Sigma can be broken down into two sub methodologies.

- **DMAIC** (Define, Measure, Analyze, Improve and Control)
- **DMADV** (Define, Measure, Analyze, Design and Verify)

Below are the key aspects of why Lean Six Sigma strategy should be considered by the industries. It will benefit more than other business improvement methodologies and total quality management:

- **Tools and techniques:** A specific set of tools and analytical techniques that are used to identify and solve the problems.
- **Process and methodology:** Six Sigma focuses on the root problem and solves it by integrating both human aspects (cultural change, training, customer focus, etc.,) and process aspects (stability of the process, reduce variation, capability, etc) of the continuous improvement.
- **Mindset and Culture:** Six Sigma creates a powerful thinking process that relies on data and operational achievement goals with continuous detection and improvement. An improvement process does not produce the desired result unless it includes accurate tools and techniques that define the activities of the process steps. And thereafter the methodology insists on a systematic database approach to solve the problem.

Mostly research suggests that entrepreneurs who implement six sigma methodology generate a 40% higher ROI as compared to those who adopt other methodologies. Since this methodology focuses on removing defects, your customers get a flawless product and a great product experience. This improves customer satisfaction. If you can deliver a great product experience consistently, you can turn your new customers into loyal customers as they keep coming back to your brand when they must purchase a product. What's more, these satisfied customers will serve as brand advocates, sharing their positive experience with your products with the world.

One of the worst things about defective processes is that they cost you money. With zero tolerance for faulty processes and products, Six Sigma drastically reduces the number of defects to 3.4 defects per million opportunities. This means that you will have to spend fewer resources on fixing glitches. Fewer defective product units also translate into less wastage. Combine that with improvement in overall quality and higher revenue and you will earn more and spend less with lean six sigma.

Managing resources efficiently especially, when you have a large workforce spread across different geographical locations can be a daunting challenge. You can get over this challenge by using Six Sigma as it focuses on metrics such as time spent on activities. This helps you to identify your biggest productivity killers, which are having a negative impact on your productivity.

In a lean six sigma environment, employees set SMART goals. SMART stands for Specific, Measurable, Attainable, Relevant and Time-bound. Employees start to critically analyze their day to day activities and identify activities they are spending their time on. This allows them to keep distractions at bay and stay focused on the goal. This helps them manage their time more efficiently.

Time is one of the three key constraints of the project management triangle alongside, scope and cost. The longer your project takes to complete the more money it will cost. To complete your project before the deadline and inside the allocated budget, you will have to reduce the project lifecycle time. This is exactly what lean six sigma helps you achieve. Create multiple teams with each team containing members from all the functional units of your organization and assign them a task to identify roadblocks that can hamper your project progress. Once they have identified the root cause of the problem, they must propose solutions to these problems. This will help you to shorten the project lifecycle.

Empower your employees or teammates by organizing six sigma training. This will broaden their horizon and help them learn new tools and techniques. Provide them with career growth opportunities so they can easily climb the corporate ladder. This not only motivates the employees but also satisfies them. When your employees are satisfied, they deliver their best.

Six Sigma is not just a methodology that helps in improving your business processes. It can also assist you with strategic planning. The key to success is to align your lean six sigma efforts with your organization's strategic goals. This gives you direction and helps your team stay focused so you can achieve your departmental goals. The same happens with other functional units. When all the functional units successfully achieve their goals, the organization thrives. What is your biggest reason for adopting lean six sigma? Let us know in the comments section below.

The essence of Six Sigma is business transformation and change. When a faulty or inefficient process is removed, it calls for a change in the work practice and employee approach. A robust culture of flexibility and responsiveness to changes in procedures can ensure streamlined project implementation. The people and departments involved should be able to adapt to change with ease, so to facilitate this, processes should be designed for quick and seamless adoption. Ultimately, the company that has an eye fixed on the data examines the bottom line periodically and adjusts its processes where necessary, can gain a competitive edge.

CHAPTER TWELVE

Pareto analysis to achieve maximum benefits

Pareto analysis is a technique used for business decision-making, but which also has applications in several different fields from welfare economics to quality control. It is based largely on the "80-20 rule." As a decision-making technique, Pareto analysis statistically separates a limited number of input factors—either desirable or undesirable—which have the greatest impact on an outcome. Pareto analysis is premised on the idea that 80% of a project's benefit can be achieved by doing 20% of the work—or, conversely, 80% of problems can be traced to 20% of the causes. Pareto analysis is a powerful quality and decision-making tool. In the most general sense, it is a technique for getting the necessary facts needed for setting priorities.

These are some business and marketing examples:

- 80% of complaints come from 20% of customers.
- 80% of profits come from 20% of the company's effort.
- 80% of sales come from 20% of products or services.
- 80% of sales are made by 20% of sellers.
- 80% of clients come from 20% of marketing activities.

Modern-day applications of Pareto analysis are used to determine which issues cause the most problems within different departments, organizations, or sectors of a business. Typically, Pareto analysis is employed by business managers, whose approach typically involves conducting a statistical analysis, such as a cause and effect analysis, to produce a list of potential problems and the outcomes of these problems. Following the information provided by the cause and effect analysis, the 80-20 rule can be applied. Here are some scenarios relevant to businesses where Pareto analysis might be applicable:

- Sharing information about defects/errors with high priority stakeholders
- Prioritizing defects or tasks according to their severity, i.e. according to their impact on a system or business
- Analyzing data or errors/defects

Making a Pareto chart

There are several ways to conduct a Pareto analysis, and they all revolve around the same guiding principles. According to the website Mind Tools, these are the six steps to conduct a Pareto analysis:

1. **Identify and list the problems.** Write a list of all the problems you need to resolve.
2. **Identify the root causes.** Determine the fundamental cause of each problem.
3. **Score the problems.** The scoring method used will depend on the type of problem. If the problem revolves around improving profits, then the scoring might center on how much each problem is costing your business. If you are trying to boost customer satisfaction, you might score the problems on the number of complaints that would be eliminated if the problem were solved.
4. **Group the problems.** Organize the problems by root cause.
5. **Tally the scores.** Add up the scores for each cause group. The group with the top score should be the highest priority, while the one with the lowest score should be the lowest priority.
6. **Take action.** Start tackling the causes of the problems. Deal with the top-priority problem or group of problems first.

Steps of Analysis

By applying the 80-20 rule, problems can be sorted based on whether they affect profits, customer complaints, technical issues, product defects, or delays and backlogs from missed deadlines. Each of these issues is given a rating based on the amount of revenue or sales, and time lost, or the number of complaints received. Here is a basic breakdown of the steps of Pareto analysis:

1. Identify the problem or problems
2. List or identify the cause of the issues or problems, noting that there could be multiple causes
3. Score the problems by assigning a number to each one that prioritizes the problem based on the level of negative impact on the company
4. Organize the problems into groups, such as customer service or system issues
5. Develop and implement an action plan, focusing on the higher scored problems first, in order to solve the problems

Not all problems will have a high score, and some smaller problems may not be worth pursuing initially. By allocating resources to high-impact issues or higher scores, companies can solve problems more efficiently by targeting the issues that have a major impact on profits, sales, or customers.

In the most general sense, the advantage of Pareto analysis is that it helps to identify and determine the root causes of defects or problems. It also helps to save time by focusing on the root causes of the problem at hand. In business, the most important resource is time and due to time, the goals usually are not to eliminate or maximize but rather to optimize. And the Pareto rule helps with optimization. Hence, businesses are able to resolve defects or errors with the highest priority first. Pareto charts can specifically help determine the cumulative impact of a problem. Cumulative impact results from effects caused by a problem happening over a long period of time. Pareto charts are especially useful for businesses or organizations because they can use them to plan the measures or actions that need to be taken in order to amend the problems. For this reason, Pareto charts can sharpen problem-solving and decision-making skills: problems related to a defect or error can be distilled into cohesive facts.

It's important to note that Pareto analysis does not provide solutions to issues, but only helps businesses to identify and narrow down the most significant causes of the majority of their problems. Once the causes have been identified, the company must then create strategies to address those problems. Pareto analysis will typically show that a disproportionate improvement can be achieved by ranking various causes of a problem and by concentrating on those solutions or items with the largest impact. The basic premise is that not all inputs have the same or even proportional impact on a given output. This type of decision-making can be used in many fields of endeavor, from government policy to individual business decisions.

Pareto analysis is used to identify problems or strengths within an organization. As an overwhelming amount of impact is often tied to a relatively smaller proportion of a company, Pareto analysis strives to identify the more material issues worth resolving or the more successful aspects of a business.

Pareto Chart Different From a Standard Vertical Bar Graph

A vertical bar graph is a type of graph that visually displays data using vertical bars going up from the bottom. In a vertical bar graph, the lengths are proportional to the quantities they represent. Vertical bar graphs are typically utilized when one axis cannot have a numerical scale. A Pareto chart is a type of chart that contains both bars and a line graph, where individual values are represented in descending order by bars, and the cumulative total is represented by the line. A Pareto chart is different from a vertical bar graph because the bars are positioned in order of decreasing height, with the tallest bar on the left.

Example of Pareto Analysis

Imagine a hypothetical example where a company is analyzing why its products are being shipped late. It comes up with 20 various reasons on what may be causing the delay. Pareto analysis holds the claim that of those 20 various reasons, roughly four of those items will be the primary cause of roughly 80% of the shipping delays. The company undertakes an analysis to track how many instances of each reason occurs. Pareto analysis isn't exact; the company may find that five reasons are causing 75% of the company's delays. Still, in principle, the fact remains that only several items are the primary drivers for a majority of outcomes. The company must focus its resources on these five reasons to make the most impactful positive change to its delivery processes.

When there seems to be too many options to choose from or its difficult to assess what is most important within a company, Pareto analysis attempts to identify the more crucial and impactful options. The analysis helps identify which tasks hold the most weight as opposed to which tasks have less of an impact. By leveraging Pareto analysis, a company can more efficiently and effectively approach its decision-making process.

CHAPTER THIRTEEN

A Spiritual Growth mindset

A spiritual Growth mindset supports the intention to lead a soulfully conscious life. Now that you are awakening in consciousness, you would like to view life with a spiritually aligned lens. Usually people understand mindset as a set of beliefs or attitude. The beliefs let you frame the situation that you are in. They determine your perception, of how you see things. Whether you interpret things to be positive or negative, your mindset has a huge part to play in it. A spiritual mindset is not just about having a set of uplifting beliefs. Rather, it also refers to a set of spiritually aligned beliefs that influence your reactions and behavior. Your mindset is a frame of mind that helps you move towards a set of outcomes. Your beliefs are framed by your awareness of your spiritual nature. They guide you in terms of making conscious choices that support your growth. There is another mindset that is even more significant and powerful than a growth mindset, one that will fundamentally impact every aspect of your life if you will embrace it: a spiritual growth mindset. When we have a spiritual growth mindset, our growth is directed toward the very specific end of becoming perfect like our loved ones, so that we can obtain exaltation and eternal life and live with Them—and our families—forever. When we adopt a spiritual growth mindset, we do more than simply acquire or develop new skills.

Many people struggle because they fail to examine the beliefs that they had unconsciously created or made in the past. Problems arise when they identify with mistaken ideas. If you are hoping to discover your true nature or find out who you really are (the "I" or "I am"), you will need to shed off the layers of untruths. These untruths are likely to prevent you from reaching your highest potential.

When something undesirable happens in your life, take it as a test. Challenge yourself to not harbor negativity and respond in a positive way. Practice controlling your thoughts to generate a good outcome. Every one of us has enemies and makes bad decisions, and sometimes evil situations happen, but spiritual progress comes from seeing these situations as a learning experience to grow. Happiness does not come from any material belonging or another person. We think our happiness comes from fulfilling a desire. Living in this mentality is like sweet poison, because once we attain our desires, it's finished, and then our soul creates another one. The problem arises when the pleasure ends and the soul continually tries to create more desires that will not last. It's like trying to quench a fire with oil—the more you satiate it, the bigger it gets.

The solution is to understand that the happiness you are seeking is not in the desire. Turn inward instead of outward. We are careless with our thought process by harboring hatred, envy, resentment, and fear. These are unwholesome thoughts because they are not healthy for us. Start to practice the reverse of these thoughts to neutralize them. Our repetitive thoughts have created channels in our minds that are unproductive. We analyze our situations and we analyze our lives to a nauseating level.

We are governed by our habits. Cutting these undesirable habits is not easy, but when we start thinking good of others, giving others the benefit of the doubt, and being kind, you will see your life quickly change. Our thoughts, ideas, beliefs, aspirations, and attachments are what causes tension in our minds. How do we purify our minds while living amid chaos and turmoil? Maybe to some, it is a simple gesture of allowing your mind to go quiet and speaking to God. To others, it may be simplifying your life of material things. Some people may find comfort in meditation and fasting. Finding that place of peace in your mind with the utmost faith in a positive outcome is a detachment from the material environment. After all, you are truly the only one who can break your heart.

Mindset is something that all great educator, successful entrepreneurs, thought leaders and Olympic athletes have. They have mindset coaches to help them achieve higher and higher breakthroughs. For support, they also surround themselves with mentors, peers and team members with a positive growth mentality. It is how glass ceilings are shattered and new records are broken every other day. In my opinion, more than just accolades, true success has to incorporate spirituality. Thus, making the choice to view and approach life from a spiritual angle, would involve developing a spiritual mindset. A spiritual growth mindset sets you up with true success in the world.

There are energy tools and visualization methods that you can use for leveraging the power of your mind. A spiritual growth mindset is developed through a process of up-levelling and alchemy. You make it a consistent practice and applying follow throughs in your everyday life. It involves mindfulness, directing your thoughts and with awareness about Universal laws, such as the Law of Attraction, Law of Karma, Law of Non-attachment and so on. Tapping into the power of a Spiritual Growth Mindset, you work on manifesting success that is aligned with your soul purpose.

I believe this issue of stuckness is a mindset matter, and your mindset has everything to do with your journey. The spiritual growth mindset understands we will face obstacles and challenges along the way, but we can be confident we will overcome the challenges – faith in the process. When you have God-confidence, you are open to learning new things (you are fearless) in order to achieve your goals. Women with God-confidence exhibit perseverance and the "stick-to-itiveness" needed to overcome.

Mindfulness is the state of being conscious and aware of what is happening both within and around you. Practicing this mindset helps you stay positive, prevent obsessing over potential problems and lead a meaningful life. As you learn to regulate your emotions in this manner, you can minimize the risk of experiencing stress, anxiety, and depression. Mindfulness can be practiced in both formal and informal ways. Formal mindfulness meditation can involve a focus on the breath and the 5 senses. Another way to practice mindfulness is to focus on one activity at a time. For example, you can focus on the act of walking, working, or simply cleaning. By focusing on mindfulness, over time, you'll notice that you feel more peaceful and content.

It's easy to dwell on negative emotions or obsess over negative thoughts if you're not intentional in being aware of what is working in your life. One way to focus on your blessings is to keep a gratitude journal. Make it a habit to list down a few things you are grateful for each day. This will let you realize all of the good things in your life and help you become optimistic and content.

Many people are still having trouble coping with the negative effects of the pandemic, and one of these is not being able to go out as freely as possible due to the fear of the virus. Feeling this way is understandable and normal. While you can't always control the world around you, you are still in charge of your environment at home. Because of this, nurture a peaceful haven in your house that allows you to ease your worries, let go of stress, and simply unwind. This might be a reading nook, a spot in the dining room where you burn incense and meditate, or a corner of your yard filled with colorful flowers.

Your inner voice can be your worst enemy. While that little voice in your head throws the harshest criticisms on you, it can become your biggest ally and friend with some practice. The key here is to make peace with it. For instance, if it says you aren't good enough, consider taking this as an opportunity to determine why you feel that way. See if you can use your negative thinking habits to strengthen yourself.

Developing ourselves as a spiritual being has enormous benefits as it helps us bring meaning into our life, leading to greater happiness. Furthermore, spiritual awakening also helps to experience more compassion and gratitude, resulting in a higher capacity to handle stress. Additionally, it allows us to forge and grow in positive relationships and social connections. Spirituality is a way of life that enables us to find joy and inspiration around us. When we believe in an energy/power greater than us, we also understand that we do not have to carry the emotional burden alone. One can let go of baggage and experience peace of mind which comes with being more mindful of our existence.

Spirituality has the immense ability to enhance our human experience. Furthermore, it may serve as a support system of inner guidance and self-discovery if you are struggling and unable to find meaning or connect to your surroundings. Or, perhaps you find yourself constantly giving into the pressure of comparing your life with that of others, resulting in dissatisfaction and the loss of any meaningful fulfilment in your life. And make you lose touch with your inner spark and dreams. Therapy for spiritual struggles, like all therapy, happens in a safe space where you will be supported and guided by a trained psychologist. Spirituality has the power to change your life for the better. As you follow these suggestions, you can take steps toward enhancing your well-being. Best of all, you give yourself a chance to become empowered, focus on your personal growth, and renew a sense of belongingness in the world. To start taking charge of the way you think, talk, and act and explore spirituality further, consult a mental health counsellor.

CHAPTER FOURTEEN

Transformational management style

The primary goals of transformational leadership are to inspire growth, promote loyalty, and instill confidence in group members. Transformational Leadership is defined as a leadership approach that causes change in individuals, teams, organizations and social systems. It creates valuable and positive change in individuals with the end goal of developing them into leaders. Enacted in its authentic form, Transformational Leadership enhances the motivation, morale and performance of people through a variety of mechanisms. These include connecting the individual's sense of identity and self to the mission and the collective identity of the organization; being a role model for others; challenging individuals and teams to take greater ownership and accountability for their work, and understanding the strengths and weaknesses of themselves. In doing so the Transformational Leader can align individuals, teams and the organization with tasks that optimize their performance.

Transformational leaders are constantly open to innovation wherever it may arise. They constantly look for opportunities to do things differently and are always open to new ideas, no matter where those ideas may present themselves. Often involves shifting people's views on how things should work. To do so, it's necessary to understand the rationale behind people's current mindsets and how to shift their thinking. The transformational leader needs to understand where people are coming from and convince them to step outside of their comfort zone. This requires two separate skills: empathy and the ability to inspire confidence. It's not enough for transformational leaders to request — or even inspire — ideas. They also need to make their colleagues and team members feel bold enough to share those ideas. Transformational leaders hear ideas with an open mind and respond without judgment or finality. They commit to employing active listening techniques so that their team members feel seen, understood and respected. With these methods in place, they inspire others to share their thoughts without self-censoring. No transformation happens without some risk of failure. A transformational leader needs to be willing to consider those risks and what they might mean for the future of the organization. If the benefits of an idea outweigh the risks, the leader must be willing to pursue it further if it seems feasible. The leader also has to recognize when the risk is too great, and a different approach is needed. Any innovator who ventures into uncharted territory must be willing to own the results of doing so, good or bad. No leader inspires confidence if they demand that others take the fall when an idea fails. Transformational leaders must assume responsibility for each of their decisions, including green lighting the ideas of others. People need autonomy to develop and shape new ideas. The transformational leader understands this and trusts team members to define their own steps to success. For innovation to happen, it needs to be part of a team's culture. The transformational leader needs to expect creativity from everyone — not just one or two "idea people." The leader's job is to model universal creativity and innovation. There needs to be an established expectation that everyone — including the leader — will think outside the box, recognizing thoughts and ideas, even when they don't generate paradigm-shifting results. Transformational leaders create transformational teams where everyone is an idea person.

There are many kinds of leadership styles. While some may benefit the individual leader or offer short-term results, transformational leadership inspires actions and habits designed to help an organization over long time periods. This approach has gained popularity because it can be the proverbial win-win, helping both the leader and organization succeed. For example, rather than focus on tactics or short-term issues, a transformational leader gives priority to understanding what motivates individual employees and helps them focus on the company's long-term vision. These leaders also aren't afraid to be challenged or consider constructive criticism. As a result, employees are empowered to share their ideas and offer constructive criticism of new directives. Leaders will also take risks and encourage suggestions from others so everyone has input into the team's accomplishments. Rather than a rigid leadership approach, transformational leaders practice team building and encourage coaching. Building confidence in employees' ability to succeed and learn from failures better prepares organizations for sudden changes, such as a reorganization or downsizing.

Transformational leaders not only challenge the status quo they also boost creativity among followers. The leader boosts followers to explore new ways of doing things and new opportunities to learn.

Transformational leadership also involves supporting and inspiring individual followers. To foster supportive relationships, transformational leaders keep lines of communication open so that followers feel free to share ideas and so that leaders can offer immediate recognition of the unique contributions of each follower.

Acquiring communication skills such as resolving workplace conflicts and recognizing employees' needs are important parts of transformational leadership. Such programs can serve as essential parts of health promotion efforts in the workplace to help improve employee well-being.

Transformational leaders have a clear vision that they can articulate to followers. These leaders can also help followers experience the same passion and motivation to fulfill these goals.

The transformational leader serves as a role model for followers. Because followers trust and respect the leader, they emulate this individual and internalize their ideals.

Those led by transformational individuals have better performance and are more satisfied than those in groups with different types of leaders. Employees who identified a higher level of transformational leadership in their employers also reported higher levels of well-being. The effect stayed significant even after researchers controlled for factors linked to well-being, such as job strain, education, and age. This is attributed to the fact that transformational leaders believe that their followers can do their best, leading group members to feel inspired and empowered.

The best way to impart inspirational motivation to employees is to positively model it. Transformational leaders serve as role models for employees in every way. That also includes modeling ethical and socially desirable behavior, maintaining a dedication to work goals and exhibiting enthusiasm about company strategy. The foundation of this influence is trust and respect. Leaders who have developed idealized influence are trusted and respected by employees to make good decisions, and not just for the good of the organization, but for the good of the team and for them as individuals. With this trust, employees become followers who want to emulate their leaders and internalize their ideals.

A transformational leader:

- Is a model of integrity and fairness.
- Sets clear goals.
- Has high expectations.
- Encourages others.
- Provides support and recognition.
- Stirs the emotions of people.
- Gets people to look beyond their self-interest.
- Inspires people to reach for the improbable.

Transformation Leadership in the workplace involves long-term, self-regulating, disciplined activities. These are above and beyond specific external rewards and are themselves of value to each individual. For Transformation Leadership to be sustained within an organization there must be a long-term dedication to vision, ideals, skills, energy, application, creativity, review and renewal. The Transformation Leadership within an organization always remains with the transformational process of the individual. Learn the power of positive change in your organization and how to develop the characteristic behaviors of a transformational leader that can drive success, while gaining the techniques that inspire teams to create bold new visions.

Create A United Future view

We are facing unprecedented challenges everyday– social, economic and environmental driven by accelerating globalization and a faster rate of technological developments. At the same time, those forces are providing us with countless new opportunities for human advancement. The future is uncertain and we cannot predict it but we need to be open and ready for it. You can prepare yourself and your teammates for jobs that have not yet been created, for technologies that have not yet been invented, to solve problems that have not yet been anticipated. It will be a shared responsibility to seize opportunities and find solutions. To navigate through such uncertainty, students will need to develop curiosity, imagination, resilience and self-regulation they will need to respect and appreciate the ideas, perspectives and values of others and they will need to cope with failure and rejection, and to move forward in the face of adversity. Their motivation will be more than getting a good job and a high income; they will also need to care about the well-being of their friends and families, their communities and the planet.

The aim of the project is to help countries find answers to two far-reaching questions:

• What knowledge, skills, attitudes and values will today's leaders need to thrive and shape their world?

• How can instructional systems develop these knowledge, skills, attitudes and values effectively?

A Shared Vision

You are committed to helping every teammates develop as a whole person, fulfil his or her potential and help shape a shared future built on the well-being of individuals, communities and the planet.

Teammates joined recently will need to abandon the notion that resources are limitless and are there to be exploited; they will need to value common prosperity, sustainability and well-being. They will need to be responsible and empowered, placing collaboration above division, and sustainability above short-term gain.

In the face of an increasingly volatile, uncertain, complex and ambiguous world, training can make the difference as to whether people embrace the challenges they are confronted with or whether they are defeated by them. And in an era characterized by a new explosion of scientific knowledge and a growing array of complex societal problems, it is appropriate that curricula should continue to evolve, perhaps in radical ways.

Need for new solutions and action plan for your growth in a rapidly changing world

- Societies are changing rapidly and profoundly
- Climate change and the depletion of natural resources, need analysis of impacts in your industry.
- Scientific and technological knowledge is creating new opportunities and solutions that can enrich our lives, while at the same time fuelling disruptive waves of change in every sector. Unprecedented innovation in science and technology, especially in bio-technology and artificial intelligence, is raising fundamental questions about what it is to be human. It is time to create new economic, social and institutional models that pursue better lives for all.
- Financial interdependence at local, national and regional levels has created global value chains and a shared economy, but also pervasive uncertainty and exposure to economic risk and crises. Data is being created, used and shared on a vast scale, holding out the promise of expansion, growth and improved efficiency while posing new problems of cyber security and privacy protection
- As the global population continues to grow, migration, urbanization and increasing social and cultural diversity are reshaping countries and communities.
- In large parts of the world, inequalities in living standards and life chances are widening, while conflict, instability and inertia, often intertwined with populist politics, are eroding trust and confidence in government itself. At the same time, the threats of war and terrorism are escalating.

These global trends are already affecting individual lives, and may do so for decades to come. They have triggered a global debate that matters to every country, and call for global and local solutions.

Need for broader goals: Individual and collective well-being

Unless steered with a purpose, the rapid advance of science and technology may widen inequities, exacerbate social fragmentation and accelerate resource depletion. In the 21st century, that purpose has been increasingly defined in terms of well-being. But well-being involves more than access to material resources, such as income and wealth, jobs and earnings, and housing. It is also related to the quality of life, including health, civic engagement, social connections, education, security, life satisfaction and the environment. Equitable access to all of these underpins the concept of inclusive growth.

You and Your Teammate Development has a vital role to play in developing the knowledge, skills, attitudes and values that enable people to contribute to and benefit from an inclusive and sustainable future. Learning to form clear and purposeful goals, work with others with different perspectives, find untapped opportunities and identify multiple solutions to big problems will be essential in the coming years.

Navigating through a complex and uncertain world

Future ready leaders need to exercise activity, in their own education and throughout life. Activity implies a sense of responsibility to participate in the world and, in so doing, to influence people, events and circumstances for the better. Organizations require the ability to frame a guiding purpose and identify actions to achieve a goal. To help enable agency, educators must not only recognise learners' individuality, but also acknowledge the wider set of relationships – with their trainers, peers, families and communities – that influence their learning. A concept underlying the learning framework is co-agency the interactive, mutually supportive relationships that help learners to progress towards their valued goals. In this context, everyone should be considered a learner, not only students but also teachers, school managers, parents and communities. Two factors, in particular, help learners enable agency. The first is a personalised learning environment that supports and motivates each teammate to nurture his or her passions, make connections between different learning experiences and opportunities, and design their own learning projects and processes in collaboration with others. The second is building a solid foundation: literacy and numeracy remain crucial. In the era of digital transformation and with the advent of big data, digital literacy and data literacy are becoming increasingly essential, as are physical health and mental well-being.

Need for a broad set of knowledge, skills, attitudes and values in action

Teammates who are best prepared for the future are change agents. They can have a positive impact on their surroundings, influence the future, understand others' intentions, actions and feelings, and anticipate the short and long-term consequences of what they do.

The concept of capability implies more than just the acquisition of knowledge and skills; it involves the mobilization of knowledge, skills, attitudes and values to meet complex demands. Future-ready professionals will need both broad and specialised knowledge. Disciplinary knowledge will continue to be important, as the raw material from which new knowledge is developed, together with the capacity to think across the boundaries of disciplines and "connect the dots". Epistemic knowledge, or knowledge about the disciplines. Procedural knowledge is acquired by understanding how something is done or made – the series of steps or actions taken to accomplish a goal. Some procedural knowledge is domain-specific, some transferable across domains. It typically develops through practical problem-solving, such as through design thinking and systems thinking.

The use of this broader range of knowledge and skills will be mediated by attitudes and values (e.g. motivation, trust, respect for diversity and virtue). The attitudes and values can be observed at personal, local, societal and global levels. While human life is enriched by the diversity of values and attitudes arising from different cultural perspectives and personality traits, there are some human values (e.g. respect for life and human dignity, and respect for the environment, to name two) that cannot be compromised.

Creating new value: New sources of growth are urgently needed to achieve stronger, more inclusive and more sustainable development. Innovation can offer vital solutions, at affordable cost, to economic, social and cultural dilemmas. Innovative economies are more productive, more resilient, more adaptable and better able to support higher living standards. To prepare for 2030, people should be able to think creatively, develop new products and services, new jobs, new processes and methods, new ways of thinking and living, new enterprises, new sectors, new business models and new social models. Increasingly, innovation springs not from individuals thinking and working alone, but through cooperation and collaboration with others to draw on existing knowledge to create new knowledge. The constructs that underpin the competency include adaptability, creativity, curiosity and open-mindedness.

Reconciling tensions and dilemmas: In a world characterized by inequities, the imperative to reconcile diverse perspectives and interests, in local settings with sometimes global implications, will require young people to become adept at handling tensions, dilemmas and trade-offs, for example, balancing equity and freedom, autonomy and community, innovation and continuity, and efficiency and the democratic process. Striking a balance between competing demands will rarely lead to an either/or choice or even a single solution. Individuals will need to think in a more integrated way that avoids premature conclusions and recognises interconnections. In a world of interdependency and conflict, people will successfully secure their own well-being and that of their families and their communities only by developing the capacity to understand the needs and desires of others. To be prepared for the future, individuals have to learn to think and act in a more integrated way, taking into account the interconnections and inter-relations between contradictory or incompatible ideas, logics and positions, from both short- and long-term perspectives. In other words, they have to learn to be systems thinkers.

Taking responsibility: The third transformative competency is a prerequisite of the other two. Dealing with novelty, change, diversity and ambiguity assumes that individuals can think for themselves and work with others. Equally, creativity and problem-solving require the capacity to consider the future consequences of one's actions, to evaluate risk and reward, and to accept accountability for the products of one's work. This suggests a sense of responsibility, and moral and intellectual maturity, with which a person can reflect upon and evaluate his or her actions in light of his or her experiences, and personal and societal goals, what they have been taught and told, and what is right or wrong. Acting ethically implies asking questions related to norms, values, meanings and limits, such as: What should I do? Was I right to do that? Where are the limits? Knowing the consequences of what I did, should I have done it? Central to this competency is the concept of self-regulation, which involves self-control, self-efficacy, responsibility, problem solving and adaptability. Advances in developmental neuroscience show that a second burst of brain plasticity takes place during adolescence, and that the brain regions and systems that are especially plastic are those implicated in the development of self-regulation. Adolescence can now be seen as a time not just of vulnerability but of opportunity for developing a sense of responsibility.

These transformative competencies are complex; each competency is intricately inter-related with the others. They are developmental in nature, and thus learnable. The ability to develop competencies is itself something to be learned using a sequenced process of reflection, anticipation and action. Reflective practice is the ability to take a critical stance when deciding, choosing and acting, by stepping back from what is known or assumed and looking at a situation from other, different perspectives. Anticipation mobilizes cognitive skills, such as analytical or critical thinking, to foresee what may be needed in the future or how actions taken today might have consequences for the future. Both reflection and anticipation are precursors to responsible actions.

Guiding principles:

- Clear definition: Does the construct have a commonly used and understood definition?
- Relevant for 2030: Does the construct, alone or in combination with others, equip people for future challenges?
- Interdependent: Can we say how the construct develops in conjunction with others?
- Impactful: Is the construct proven to have a bearing on future life outcomes?
- Malleable: Can the construct be developed through the processes of learning?
- Measurable: Can the construct be given a comparative numerical value on a scale, or a non-numerical account?

CHAPTER SIXTEEN

Management lessons from ancient history

Management is a concept that is centuries old and has developed with the civilizations of the world. India is treasured as a civilization that has been shaping the world for thousands of years. The concept 'management' is not new to India. Contrary to the popular belief that the topic 'management', the way it is being known and practiced today, originated in the west and progressed to the east; the subject management has always been preached and practiced

since the time of puranas in India. Indian Management reflects the ethos, beliefs and intellect of ancient Indian culture. The tradition of Indian ethos goes back to more than 3500 years, way before the days when modern management took root. Management had its stronghold since ancient Harrapan period, and has been a continuous process and is still in its development stage. When it comes to management styles, there are many like democratic, autocratic, consultative, persuasive, and finally chaotic. Managers of today are mostly focused on profit and business without taking human values, morality and the society into consideration. Ancient Indian Management systems were designed keeping the sustainability of the planet and then business values were developed and delivered to the masses by the religious preachers and became a part of our life style. Even today, India has an insignificant ecological foot-print on the planet- Thanks to our value-based management system driven life style. The amount of waste, western advanced countries produce, developing countries like India can feed a huge percentage of her population from that waste. The objection is not on their luxurious lifestyle, but those countries which cannot afford their luxurious life-style, cannot succeed economically and socially by following their management techniques. We, as Indians have a unique living style and social system which needs the support of her own economic and business management system to develop an efficient society and economy. But we are following the management techniques of the western countries which are richer than us in resources. This irony will take the country downward. Hence, we should bring changes to the management courses and produce such managers who are skilled to work in our economy as per our needs. Another side effect of this blind race can be brain drain also, which can be discussed later in due course of time

Mahabharata - This was a war that was fought between two groups - Two brothers for the throne of Hastinapur. This text holds a lot of lessons, ethics and values that we can learn and make our lives what we wish for. The Pandavas who were very few in numbers defeated the mighty Kauravas with the help of sheer determination, Planning, and proper management of their units. The leader of Kauravas has been portrayed as a very destructive person and because of his arrogance, pride and incapability of taking decisions, he led his entire clan into destruction and wrath. His side had a lot of differences among themselves and they lacked unity. Pandavas, on the other side were having a common purpose, and there was a unity for that purpose. Moreover, strategies laid down by Lord Krishna was a cherry on the cake.

Lessons from Mahabharata for a management:

Mahabharatha as a motivational source for every individual gave lessons of management to maintain any organization. From Mahabharatha we can learn the following lessons:

- Leadership: From the epic of Mahabharata we can observe the leadership style of Krishna which is a strategic.
- Administration: By observing the administrative style of Dhuryodana we can learn the lesson that all the citizens under a single administration is equal and it is the basic responsibility of a ruler to make an effective administration.
- Tactics: From observing the Mahabharata we can learn how to be tactical in various situations.
- Psychology: From Mahabharata we can learn psychology that how accesses a person and react according to the situation. These lessons also give a path about how to make decisions i.e. decision making.
- Trust and human relations: From the lessons of Mahabharata and Geeta we can learn about trust and human relations. These lessons are by

observing the characters like Arjuna and Krishna, Dhuryodhana and Karna

Ramayana - The story of a righteous man who is on a journey to find his wife who has been kidnapped by the demon king Ravana. It was his policy of 'Dharma" - Righteousness throughout his journey that has set an example of what an ideal man is. Lord Ram travelled across India leaving his comfort zone and struggled for 14 years leading an army of Monkeys to defeat the demon king. His story is full of the incidents that he faced and he manages everything without a single thought of "adharma" - un-righteousness.

Lessons of management:

1. Transformational leadership: Burns (1978) characterized transformational leadership as a process that motivates followers by appealing to higher ideals and moral values. From Ramayana Rama showed his transformational leadership by motivating his team for achieving greatest things.

2. Idealized influence: We can learn about the idealized influence from the people of Ayodhya those who believe their king Rama and followed him in all aspects of their life.

3. Intellectual simulation: We can learn the intellectual simulation from Rama who made Bharatha to think about the things which he had never questioned before.

4. Inspirational motivation: From Ramayana we can learn inspirational motivation by observing the conversation between Rama and Hanuman who got motivated and crossed ocean.

5. Individual consideration: We can learn about individual consideration by the words of a Rama that it is my vow to provide shelter and protection to any living entity from fear, even if Ravana comes for protection

Bhagavad Gita - The Bhagavad Gita is an ancient Indian spiritual and philosophical text which is more than 5000 years old. One of the greatest contributions of India to the world is the Holy Bhagavad Gita. Bhagavad Gita means the song of spirit, the song of Lord. While a casual reading of Bhagavad Gita would leave one feeling that the book is about the personal struggles involved in engaging in warfare, the Bhagavad Gita represents much more the story of warefare. The Bhagavad Gita represents the struggles encountered by all humans in everyday activities including the struggles of leadership. The Bhagavad Gita not only provides advice to modern day leaders and but also suggests important leadership qualities.

The epic book of Bhagavad Gita has guided our personal lives and has also shaped the context of managerial decision-making and building an ethical decision-making ecosystem among Indian professionals. The principles of Bhagavad Gita reveal that managing men, money and materials in the best possible way is the most important factor for successful management. Lack of management causes disorder, chaos, confusion, wastage and destruction. Bhagavad Gita repeatedly proclaims that one must try to manage oneself. The modern management thinking of vision, leadership, motivation, excellence in work, achieving goals, giving work meaning are all well versed in the Bhagavad Gita. Among all the scriptures Bhagvad Gita is considered topmost as the supreme Lord Krishna himself is speaking and answering the questions of his devotee Arjuna.

Bhagvad Gita deals with five basic subjects.

1) Jiva :- The soul , its nature , and its situation in this material world

2) Ishwara :- The Supreme Lord , how he is always with the living entities, his creative and destructive power . He is supreme enjoyer.

3) Prakriti :- The material nature (eternal energy of lord) and the three modes of material nature

4) Kala :- Time and its effect

5) Karma :- The action and reaction cycle.

The Bhagavad Gita is the summary of all Vedic philosophies and its teachings can be effectively applied to address any problem related to individual or organisation and is a strong source of illumination. The Bhagavad Gita suggest advice's on humanistic and inclusive leadership and guides managers to seek higher level of consciousness while seeking for others influence, some most important qualities that a modern manager should follow maintaining proper role, being proactive with wisdom, self-sacrifice.

From that we can observe the characters of a leader as:

1. Visionary: a leader should think about the future problems in advance and he should be ready with the solution fro that problem.

2. Perfect analyzer: A leader should analyze his team perfectly and he has to give perfect resources according to the situation to his team.

3. Perfect planning: He should make a perfect strategy to come out of difficulties from odd situations.

4. Leader should be a team player: leader should be a team player first and should be in contact and should be available for his time in all situations

and time.

5. Knowledgeable: A leader should possess the knowledge which can make the team to face any situation at any time and at any level of source availability.

6. Leader should be a perfect councilor: Not providing resources he should be a psychological analyst and councilor for his team also. At the time of psychological distress of team members he should come to know the status and should give them moral support to his team.

7. Leader should be balanced in all situations and with all results. These words from Bhagavat Geeta say that one can get consistency of mind and action when he is balanced in his emotions, towards any result and situation

Chanakya Neeti - The book of administration, law, politics and self help too. The Chanakya Neeti also called as "Arthashastra of Kautilya" is indeed a good book for changing your perspectives on what the world actually is. Chanakya was a pioneer in the field of administration and political science. He assisted Chandragupta Maurya to his become a king and establish the Mauryan empire.

There is no friendship without self-interest: Chanakya explains that behind every friendship there is self-interest. Without it, friendship cannot last. Before you make your new friends, always ask yourself why is this person getting closer and building new relations, and trust me that would be the point. In the modern-day scenario, many people make friends and get closer to you only when they need something, otherwise, they don't, but Modernity is not the cause for all this. It is happening for a long time as it is indeed human nature. You can see this even in the story of Mahabharata between the friendship of Karna and Dhuryodhana. Both had the same motive and self-interest and that was to defeat the Pandavas.

Escaping the attitude is oneself is very ruinous. Never turn a blind eye when anyone is in danger: Chanakya says that we should not escape or run away from helping people in Trouble. He says that the escapist attitude of people is very dangerous as it only leads the Evil to do more bad again and again. Chanakya asks us not to turn a blind eye when anyone is in danger, rather we should face the danger courageously and confidently. Your fearlessness in the face of danger will reduce its impact and then finally it will lead you to overpower it.

The enemy has to be destroyed completely: Chanakya says that your enemy should be destroyed completely. Even if one-quarter of the army remained, in due course of time it could become strong, and may even retaliate. An incident occurred in Chanakya's life where the roots of the Kush plant pricked the feet of Chanakya's father and he died because of that. Chanakya decided to destroy the kush root completely from its place. Each day he used to go there and pull the plant including the root and used to pour buttermilk into it so that no new plant sprouted there. When some asked Chanakya's reason for this, he replied that "I can't bear if anything upsets humans and humanity, hence I am completely uprooting these thorns. Such was the dedication and stubbornness of Chanakya when it comes to destroying his enemies. One must always have this stubbornness and dedication in whatever task he/she takes.

Never share your secrets and goals with anybody: Chanakya says that one should not share his/her secrets with anybody because it will only lead the other person to share them with someone else. In this way, the secrets are known to everybody afterward and some may even use them to blackmail or destroy you in no time. Think about this in real-life situations where you end up sharing your secrets with someone, and that person changes sides because of some self-interest or bias, wouldn't he use your given secrets against you? Therefore you should keep your life matters to yourself.

A wise man also faces trouble if he advises a fool, if he protects an evil man, and has deals with depression: Chanakya says that a Wise man faces trouble if he advises a fool. The reason is that a fool will never agree with your sayings, the reason is that he is either brainwashed or he is capable to understand the logic. Chanakya also says not to protect an Evil man, because there is no guarantee that an Evil man would be nice to you after you protect him. Also, the protection of evil men will not solve any problems but rather will facilitate more evil. Chanakya also advises not to have any dealing with a depressed man because a depressed man by his mental conditions will surely be unable to take good decisions and will surely create confusion in the dealings without looking at the outcomes. It can only lead you in a trouble.

If one craves comfort, then he should drop the idea of studying and if one wants to study sincerely then he should stop craving comfort. One cannot get education and comfort simultaneously: In a very simple language, Chanakya says that learning cannot be done in your comfort zone. To learn something, you need to get out of your comfort/nest. You need to fail and even get humiliated, only then there is a coming of knowledge. These days students are all time in their books and some are having no practical exposure to what they are reading, it's just that they read something and they write it in their examination. Where does it end? Nowhere. Chanakya says that education and comfort cannot come simultaneously.

Control Greedy by money, The arrogant by submissiveness, the fool by preaching, and the learned by telling him the reality: Chanakya says that "Control greed by money ", he means that a greedy person will only agree with you if you win him over by giving money. Because for a greedy man there is nothing above money, give him that and he will surely take your side. Chanakya says that "The Arrogant man by submissiveness" because an arrogant man always wants himself to look superior to others. He will only listen to you when you keep yourself as empathetic and look submissive. Chanakya says "The fool by preaching" is because the fool here is someone who does not know anything about a particular topic. He will simply agree with you when you start preaching some things about the matter he does not know. Lastly when Chanakya says "a learned person by telling him the reality", it is simply because a learned person knows a particular situation and the only thing it will help you win over him is the facts and evidence.

Brilliance has the power, Physical strength does not matter: Why not? Chanakya himself was responsible for bringing an entire empire down. His plans and his strategy were the results of his brilliance and mental strength. The entire Mahabharata war was won by the Pandavas just because of the plans and brilliance of Lord Krishna and not otherwise. Therefore, Brilliance has the power, physical strength indeed matters, but then.....

What can all the scriptures do to a person, when he does not use his common sense? : Chanakya says that if a person does not use his common sense, the rules and actions laid down by scriptures are of no use to him. It's like saying that a mirror is of no use to a blind man. Everything application of knowledge requires you have common sense

Management lessons from Kautilya's Arthasastra:

Being the first Sastra about the economics of Indians Kautilya"s Arthasastra taught us every aspect of administration and management for total economy and as well as for an individual level also. Kautilya"s Arthasastra gave us lessons like:

1. Human resource management: how to select various levels of employees for an organization.

2. Resource management: it will give you total idea about allocating resources for various departments in an organization.

3. Motivational practices: it will give us total procedures and methods to be followed by an organization for motivating an employee.

4. Corporate restructuring: at the time of losses of at the time of monitory requirement we need to generate money accordingly so for generating resources and opportunities he gave total methods to follow.

5. Making alliances: while going for new markets or new places we have to know about that place particularly and all the conditions particularly for that we need to take resources from the local persons or from the persons or organizations that had resources. For that we need to combine with them so Kautilya"s Arthasastra will give us how to make deals with other companies.

6. From the Kautilya"s Arthasastra we come to know how to improve security for our territory and how to develop secret forces to improve our security

We need to implement the practices of coexistence and cohesion at the workplace (loka sagraham and samanva) and maintain a balance between pravṛtti and nivṛtti (materialism and spiritualism) for corporate prosperity. We have to merge the ecology of the soul (atma) with the ecology of the organisation to create a conscience-based management practice. Most problems in managing businesses can be answered through a thorough reading of ancient scriptures. While Thirukural has answers to issues in planning, organising, strategising and controlling, management paradigms and leadership ideas can be derived from ancient literature like Bhagavad Gita, Vedanta, Kautilaya's Arthashastra, and Panchatantra. Indian scriptures are depositories of philosophical thoughts, which play an important role in the development of indigenous psychological constructs. Constructs like manas and lajja capture cognition, emotion and behaviour; these are concepts used in modern management systems

CHAPTER SEVENTEEN

MANAGEMENT LESSONS FROM WARS IN INDIA

Throughout history, wars have left an indelible mark on human psyche. Serious debates have been held on the morality of and the strategic necessity for war. And yet, like every dark cloud that has a silver lining, wars too at times leave a society wiser. India is no stranger to wars. And there are many lessons to be learnt from each of those battles — management lessons, to be precise.

1. Battles of Tarain (1191-92 AD)
2. Battle of the Jhelum (Porus and Alexander 326 BC)
3. Battle of Saraighat (1671 AD)
4. The Battle of Talikota (1565 AD): The Fall of the Vijayanagara Empire
5. The battle of Diu (1509 AD) (The second battle of Chaul)
6. Battle of Haldighati (1576 AD)
7. Third Battle of Panipat (1761 AD)
8. The battle for Jhansi (1858 AD)
9. Battle of Aberdeen (Andaman 1859 AD)
10. The Battle of Plassey (1757 AD)

- No management should let an incident of misconduct or treason pass. Unethical conduct by any person warrants eviction. A routine step like job rotation or transfer doesn't help. An immediate disciplinary action, on the other hand, sets a precedent for others. No organisation should tolerate any behaviour not aligned with its policies.
- When one door is closed, look for another. A setback should not stop one from pursuing one's dream. One should be open to explore all opportunities at hand and try to capitalize on them. Perseverance always

pays.

- Any leader should weigh the pros and cons thoroughly before deciding on any promotion or demotion. In case a promotion/demotion is decided upon, a leader should have a well thought-out strategy to deal with others aspiring for the same position.

- In an organisation, a leader should be firm in the affairs of the state and should not tolerate any indiscipline even if the same is committed by a top ranking executive. In an age of high attrition, a leader needs to ensure that his dependence on key resources is minimal. Even if one act of treason may be forgiven, a repeat act should never ever be tolerated upon and should be punished with expulsion.

- Lack of proper training is a major disadvantage. An organisation that plans to roll out a new tool or technology should test and pilot it properly prior to implementation.

- While building a team, a manager should assign critical tasks to those who are skilled as well as trustworthy. Meetings are necessary to identify simmering issues if any.

- In the long term, unethical actions always fail, their short-term gains notwithstanding. At times, people take wrong steps, lured by chances of quick benefits. Though they realise their follies in the end, very few have the courage to admit that.

- One should explore all alternatives to achieve goals. Sometimes, alternatives may seem unacceptable but one has to make the best of the bad bargain. Whatever the alternative, a well-thought-out plan with action is always better than inaction and sheer reliance on luck.
Similarly, an organisation may be forced choose from among undesirable options like sell-off, massive retrenchment or bankruptcy.

- Who had the determination to escape, every organisation has a few 'go-getters', who can rise to any challenge. They thrive under crisis, and are willing to take on risks.

- Every organisation should have a good induction process for any new hire. It could include rigorous class-room training or an on-job training or a mix of both.

- Mission-critical plans should be known initially to a few core team members and disclosed to the full team just before execution. If one finds a potential leak in information, one should postpone, cancel or alter the plan.

- Strong initiative and capability without the moral compass is extremely dangerous. Organizations have to be on the lookout and discard such employees immediately who do not adhere to organisation's core values. Values have to be one of the essential filters while recruiting, especially senior leaders.
- Involve the team in any major decision-making process. When one has the buy-in, it yields far better results.
- Team formation is fundamental to success, and senior management involvement helps. They can apply their rich experience in choosing right people for the right job. This also helps team members to have an access with senior management if they have any suggestions and recommendations. It also makes information flow smoother and decision-making faster.
- A leader should anticipate the opponent's move and strategies accordingly. This takes the surprise factor out of the equation and helps in keeping the morale of the team high.
- Although quantity might provide an edge, quality can add to the edge. Or blunt it, at times. Informed and intelligent decision-making overcomes many apparent disadvantages. It is very easy for an organisation to relinquish market dominance due to a bad decision. Some of these decisions have quick impact, while others might become evident after some time. If time permits, one should revisit the decisions or else learn from it to avoid future mistakes.
- Opportunity comes without any announcement. It should be sensed, grabbed and exploited.
- Giving and receiving feedback is an art and should be executed carefully. Leaders should be careful in providing feedback. If feedback is not good, the leadership must provide an opportunity for another round of discussions where misgivings could be set right. Praise openly, criticize confidentially — that should be the policy with those in strategic positions.
- Any case of ethics or serious offence should be handled immediately, irrespective of employee's past performance and high rating.
- Risk and reward go hand in hand. It is human to expect appropriate reward for taking risks.
- A good leader can learn from Lakshmibai's conviction, commitment, skill, flexibility and can-do attitude. An organisation can also learn from her life: it can learn to be prepared for a topsy-turvy ride in the long

run. There could be multiple roadblocks and hiccups. But the important lesson is to learn from the losses and consolidate the wins; this will help in turning an organisation into an institution, which could be respected by all.

- One needs allies; the need is even stronger when one is operating in a new territory/segment. Whether the company is doing an acquisition or is entering into a partnership, the agreement should try to be a 'win-win' one where the minority stakeholder should feel respected and heard. This will help the partnership flourish. Similarly, if a manager takes care of his team, his team rally for him in his hour of need.

- One should learn from a setback and improve; one must have the determination to win. Sometimes, a better plan emerges that could increase the probability of success as in Abidali's case, where he saw his troops decimated on the other side of the river. Similarly, one may need to take snap decisions depending on the situation. An individual with a good network and a company that has good market intelligence can get the latest information, which could be crucial in planning and providing competitive advantage. When the stakes are high, lack of intelligence can invariably prove fatal, as in the case of how Abdali crossing the Yamuna went unnoticed by the Marathas.

- It is important to do 'what if' contingency analysis planning for various scenarios. This upfront analysis may trigger a new partnership or alignment which could benefit the company. Sometimes, one has to provide new concessions to gain the required support and solidify one's position. Both wars and businesses can benefit from a deep multi-step scenario analysis.

- Empower and trust your team members. One should have complementary skills among the senior management so that the leader can tap into a breadth of expertise. Finally, decisions are taken by the leader but an environment that encourages different voices and dissenting opinions is more effective than the 'do as I tell you to do' attitude. This is what encouraged Najib to convince Abdali. Even though Najib failed miserably in the initial phase, Abdali continued to give him a chance to prove himself. Similarly, a manager needs to have faith in his team despite early setbacks, provided they possess the right skills; after all, every mistake is a learning experience.

- One should not give up the fight till the last moment. The leader's behaviour during critical times can either motivate to overcome the challenge or lead to a psychological defeat where victory was possible. It is also important to have a backup plan that can be used if the original one is not working, as Abdali did with the reserve troops and cannons on camels. The leader should be bold in making changes in the team to ensure that a fresh mind can look into the issue from a new perspective and provide a solution, instead of the same tired mind being stuck in the same track of thought.

- To rise after a fall requires grit and determination. It is not sufficient just to learn from mistakes and take corrective action. Changing the mindset of the team from being a loser to having faith in itself is a must. Then the team will rise and face the challenge again with confidence. Projects that are failing or not doing well can be turned around by adopting this strategy.

- Prepare a backup plan to face any contingency. This plan should be executed at an appropriate time when the current plan fails to deliver the desired result. This is what Maharaja Udai Singh II had done by building a new town and seamlessly shifting the capital when Chittor fell.

- Succession planning should be reviewed periodically, and modified based on the ground realities. It should be done on merit, not on favouritism.

- One could set an aggressive goal even if it is against popular belief or practice, provided one is determined and weighs the decision well by considering the full perspective.

- Don't be rigid. One should be flexible in entertaining new ideas and suggestions from the team members, and take corrective actions if convinced.

- Leadership does not come by position, but by the qualities one demonstrates. This can turn the person into a role model, someone people would like to emulate. Here, Pratap's leadership qualities impressed Shakhti Singh, who, in turn, showed a higher sense of maturity. Bravery and leadership of Pratap appealed to his higher senses. Leadership guided by higher senses and great value systems are sustainable. It makes others follow the path.

- Willing to change the strategy by learning from the failed ones. The goal is to find a winning strategy. It's a case of using one's strength against the enemy's weakness. Lack of knowledge of the local terrain made Mughals vulnerable to guerrilla attacks that Maharana Pratap together with Bhils utilised to their advantage.

- During execution, it is sometimes common to lose sight of the goal and move away from the path and take one that is not aligned with the end goal. During this time, one needs mentors, friends and allies to provide the right guidance.
- One should not be worried about setting aggressive goals for the fear of failure. Even if one cannot achieve the entire goal, partial achievement in the right direction is far more commendable than taking an easy way out.
- One should tackle one major issue or enemy at a time rather than spread out the resources thinly to tackle multiple issues all at once. One could open multiple frontiers provided one is assured of victory; otherwise, the divide-and-rule strategy should be utilized to isolate the enemies. Similarly mergers and acquisitions of smaller competitors could pose greater threat and one needs to explore various options like preemptive acquisition, alternative markets, different product positioning or differentiated offering.
- The experience should be used in better planning based on the available resources and introspect the weak areas so that it could be covered well. The leader should put right people on the right job so that he himself can look into the bigger picture and take corrective action based on developments in the field. The leader has to groom his staff so that he can confidently delegate the next level of detail to his subordinates. The leader should avoid getting into deeper tactical details as this can distract him from focusing on the strategic goal.
- Use of superior technology can be a decisive advantage. It helps in making better competitive products and winning the market. Technology can also make company's internal processes better. Organizations should promote a culture to encourage innovation, so that they can have competitive edge against the competitors.
- The core team should be retained. If there is any difference in opinion, it should be sorted out amicably. If the issue is of improper reward and recognition and the request is significant, then it should be discussed to arrive at the common understanding but the realization should be linked with the outcome of project. This will help tying the reward with the result and to ensure that people stick till the project completion to realize the benefit.
- Any partnership plan should be formed to cover short term and long term goals. It should be strategic rather than tactical. The rule of

engagement should be discussed and a roadmap should be formed not only for achieving the common immediate goal, but for long term success. One can part ways after the goal is achieved, but the separation clause has to be clearly thought through and defined as part of the contract.

- Leader's mistake in rewarding sycophants or family members over deserving competent members could have far-reaching adverse impact on the company. This might create warring tribes inside the company and could be the cause of its downfall.

- Innovation is the key for to overcome entrenched incumbents. The advantages of installed product base and distribution channels are not sufficient to sustain the monopoly for long. Companies must innovate and sometimes cannibalize their existing product with a new one to maintain the leadership position. Otherwise, a new competitor with innovative product will suddenly capture the market.

- When the stakes are high, expect intense competition. Understanding the competition's strategy as well identifying the driver for the fight is vital. If one side is tremendously motivated to win, the other side must understand this and factor that into its strategy.

- Having the right type of resources is more important than simply having more resources. Under pressure from the management to meet hiring goals, manager sometimes lowers the quality bar and expands staff. This always backfires as it impacts productivity, team performance, and effectively dilutes product quality in addition to schedule delays. Equally important is the effective usage of available resources. As soon as the Egyptians realized that the small crafts were ineffective in fighting the Portuguese ships, they could have utilized these crafts for other purposes like night attacks, espionage, transport of goods and injured. Similarly, the available resources – if not useful for the initially planned work — should be redeployed for other productive activities

- One should know the turf where one has to play. Egyptians had done the right thing in choosing Diu – the turf they knew well. But they lacked an understanding of the competitor's product, and therefore couldn't position its product well against the competitor's. It is not true that if one dominates one market segment, one can win easily in the other segments too. This is the mistake Egyptians did when they considered only the Mediterranean-style warfare.

- Keeping the full city under control would have been a short term advantage to the Portuguese, but they maintained a minimum required presence to serve the strategic purpose of providing security to their trade route. Similarly, one should avoid the temptation of taking on more or to committing more to the customer without ascertaining whether it aligns with the strategy. If not well thought through, a company can get overextended in commitments. In the long run, this will require diversion of resources from other projects impacting them too.

- It is important to do the proper handover of the job. Job handover is more effective if the strategic knowledge and experience are also transferred This is vital in continuing the best practices.

- Organizations should undertake competitive barrier analysis, which helps them in understanding the conditions that make it difficult or impossible to compete in a given market segment. Once equipped with this information, organization will then be better prepared to take a right decision from long-term perspective. Ahom King took one defeat at face value and did not do a "deep dive" to understand the critical factors like monsoon and diseases that would have allowed him to avoid a humiliating treaty.

- Demonstrating results within a short timeframe allows a new leader to establish his credibility as shown by Lachit. People have high expectations from the new leader. If the leader fails to deliver quickly or up to their expectation, then he will have a difficult time to earn the respect. On the other hand, if the leader commits mistakes in a hurry to prove himself, this can destroy the team. So the leader has to balance these two factors with accurate assessment of the overall situation.

- Lachit has anticipated Mughals' move, kept an eye on their movements, worked out a war plan based on latest data. Most important, he kept his enemy engaged in discussions until he was prepared to take it head-on. Similarly, a great senior manager has to be a great juggler who can handle multiple tasks well, a great thinker who could anticipate and mitigate risks and a great implementer who can bring the desired results.

- Every relationship goes through its ups and downs including the supervisor- subordinate relationship. On one hand, it was good that Ahom King did not fire Lachit based on rumour but gave him a chance; but on the other the king did not trust Lachit's advice even though Lachit had demonstrated success and loyalty. A leader has to judge the quality of his team and build a strong sustainable relationship that can stand ups and downs in business situations.

- Building a high-performing team is important, but to get extraordinary results requires inspired leadership. Ability to turn the momentum is what differentiates a leader from mere managers. Leaders display confidence as well as inner conviction. A strong leader can lead a good team in delivering exceptional performance by convincing his troops that they can win in spite of seemingly insurmountable obstacles.

- Each intermediate milestone poses a new set of challenges. Upfront planning will help in realistically determining the complexity of the milestone and thereby taking a suitable execution path.

- Mind games are very important. Most of the time, in spite of having many pluses, a person can psychologically get defeated. This is where experience makes a lot of difference. A seasoned leader like Porus did not fall in such traps set up by Alexander

- Project could slip; go over budget and land up with depleted resources. This could happen when the leader and his team become complacent, have tasted multiple successes and therefore take new challenges lightly and do not spend enough time in thinking through.

- One should play by one's own strength and avoid providing opportunity to opponent to strike where one is weak. Alexander's cavalry was better and he used it well. He was weak in handling elephants therefore delayed attacking them.

- Just like Porus, one needs to learn how to negotiate from the point of weakness. Though he lost the sovereignty of the kingdom, but he started ruling a bigger one. Similarly during organization restructuring due to merger, acquisition or any internal event; a person might be relabeled at a perceived lower position but he might have more challenges. Rather than worry about the label, one should focus on content of the challenges.

- Leader should have right assessment of his team's morale, motivation and strength. A successful, but burnt-out team could not deliver the lofty goals as envisioned by the leader. It is important to do job rotation and induct new skills to undertake new challenges.

- Any agreement is possible if it's mutually beneficial and instills a feeling of a "win win" agreement, even if two parties are not at the same footing. The agreement will not sustain if one exploits one's superior status and forces it on the other. Sometimes, the superior party needs to yield more to reach an honorable agreement. If Jaichand had seen the advantage in helping Prithviraj Chauhan in defeating Gauri and keeping Chauhan's kingdom to act as a buffer state between his and Mohammad Gauri's, this would provide independence for long time to Jaichand too. Eventually even his kingdom was annexed by Gauri.

- Humanitarian help should be extended only if the recipient is not likely to become a "Bhasmasur" (who, on getting blessings from Lord Shiva, went back to destroy Shiva himself). While making an important decision of far-reaching impact, Leaders have to keep organization and team goal in mind rather than force personal preferences.

- The code of conduct, which is followed in the past, could not be assumed to be followed the same way unless there is a common understanding or a proper vigil to ensure its adherence. These common understandings happen in the case of collaboration and not amongst enemies. Organizations should not make the plan based on one-sided assumptions.

- A key distinction between a good manager from a not-so-good one is that a good manager will help his employees to realize their strength and suggest various options to overcome the disadvantages.

- If a person is determined, he can convert his weakness into strength in spite of his handicap. One can find many great companies in recent history that struggled initially as a startup but overcame the hurdles. This was due to their innovation and determination to take a dominant position in the market. The winning desire and attitude helps in overcoming a bad patch and building a dominant successful organization.

CHAPTER EIGHTEEN

Panchatantra Management Lessons

Doing business in the present economy is not so easy as we think by sitting in the AC rooms, always business gives lots of ups and downs in the due course. Today's business always gives you an ample opportunities to grow your business vertically and horizontally, and at the same time it troubles you with the lot of challenges, bargaining power of customers, bargaining power of suppliers, rivalry from existing competitors, rivalry from new entry to markets and rivalry from substitutes. The entrepreneurs and managers of today's business should be ready with the skills to tackle these challenges and also to grab the opportunities at all feasible manner. Panchtantra lessons are to tackle the challenges arises in due course of business and to make use prospective opportunities which business world though at managers. The Panchtantra is also known as a literary legacy of India, which has originated and developed the fables and stories. In such a way Panchtantra influences literary inspiration all around the world. The Panchatantra stories were written in 200 BC by Vishnu Sharma. From that time these stories have been translated into plentiful languages. With the foundation of ancient traditions, in the beginning, these Panchatantra tales were written in Sanskrit. The tales are short with the lucidity of language helping it to be simple to understand. These tales are for everybody i.e., the age is no bar. From generations to generations Panchatantra stories teaches the difference between right and wrong deeds. These tales always end with the moral giving us the life lessons to be followed in our day to day lives.

The name Panchtantra was selected with a purpose and meaning behind it. Pancha refers to five and tantra refers to strategies or principle. Thus Panchatantra comprises of five volumes with life principles. The five volumes include many stories that provide every individual a guidance concerning diverse aspects of day to day life and livelihood. Through these volumes the essential values of life are gathered and shared in form of motivating and inspiring stories.

Panchtantra teaches various facets of Human Quality Development to each individual for their personal & professional life. The lessons can be related to work, contest, supervision, diversity, harmony, unity and team building to have a peaceful and calm life at work and in personal domains. Panchtantra in an extraordinarily creative & innovative way teaches the lessons that are very much appropriate and relevant at workplace as it provides the guidance to manage resources in a better way so that there can be the finest utilization of available resources. It also provides guidance for mutual understanding between one another so that the harmonious environment can prevail. These lessons help in making a positive approach, commitment, enthusiasm, and keenness towards work for progress, achievement, and growth and for being emotionally & mentally balanced human beings. The different tantras of Panchtantra, are Mitrabedha (Loss of friends/Betrayal of friends), Kakolookiyam (Pragmatism), Mitrasamprapti (Gain of friends), Labdhapranasha (Loss of gains) and Aprikshitakaraka (Considerate Action).

The leadership in the organization should distribute responsibility among the team members equally. No individual should have more value than the same member of that group. Leadership should understand that each contribution is necessary for an outcome, no matter how small or big it is. They need to be transparent and seek input from all the members. An organization can be profitable only when all the members are placed on the same platform to perform. The favoritism leads to develop dissatisfaction among others. Leaders should be careful in their approach of awarding any employee without any reason. As per the story, the cart maker awarded the bell to the young camel without any reason, just because the young camel was his favorite. This award made the young camel developed an ego as he was the only camel to get such award. In this way, he stopped listening other colleague camels even the elder ones. This resulted in paying a high price by losing his own life. In the modern era, the gender discrimination is also an enormous problem within Indian society. Traditional practices have demoted women to secondary status within the household and workplace.

The important concepts of management i.e. training of an employee in an organization before putting him on the job. Lacking of it may create disaster situation for an organization and the management. Skills management elevates the productivity of the organization because individual employees become aware of the skills sets required for specific tasks and upgrade their skills to attain personal goals, thus, adding value to the organization. In today's culture of frequent job switch training is became the least important aspect. Even when the training is organized it is often at the diligence of the human resource department. There is a variety of training techniques available for different aspects of working. But, any type of training it includes set four steps plan. These four steps plan has proven to be very effective. These four steps of training are: • Plan • Present • Apply • Evaluate Similarly, before putting the monkey on the services of King if he would have been trained on how to operate the sword or dealing such situations the king would not have been wounded. The king and his attendant were at fault to keep the sword in a place, where it can be freely accessed by unskilled persons.

The association of a wicked person may lead to the severe problem or paying for their wrongs. Since years, friendship and love are considered the necessary aspects of a good social life. A friendship theory requires us to go beyond the boundaries of selfishness and I attitude. Although, in a relationship, there are situations of conflict but being ethical is the key element for the successful relationship building. We generally make friends at the workplace and the same can bring joy and happiness even in the most stressful environment. Healthy workplace friendships require the ability to separate personal and professional feelings, and if one cannot separate that, it will create problems not only for the individual but for the organization as a whole. When we are working together on a project, one needs to work towards the goal of the organization leaving aside their personal greed. In the era of competition, many companies are following unethical practices to earn maximum profit. A company should not have profit maximization as their central goal rather it should be customer oriented. Each company should have a code of ethics which defines the beliefs and values of the organization. Those values and beliefs should be strictly followed by each employee and all business practices. The business houses which routinely engage in unethical practices are ultimately suffering as their unethical behavior and actions are easier for the customer to take notice of likewise the papabuddi came to the notice of all the villagers about his wrong intention. If he would have followed ethics and the conduct of real friendship, they both could have good future. When taking a decision on any of the problem or aspect, one should evaluate it on the following parameters.

The importance aspect considered, considerate and coordinated actions of members of a group, community or organisation peace and sustainability. When there are two or more bosses in a department, there can be internal disputes (for example, assigning different work to one employee with the same deadline). When the bosses of a department are in disputes, they may act foolishly and may sacrifice the objectives of the department. Their different decision-making will affect the working of the other employees and the processes of that department.

One stomach two heads: explain the challenges of team management in the organisation under the team work. A story of bird having two heads with one stomach explains what should not be done in the organisation as team. Team members should have good understanding among the members. When misunderstanding arises among the team members leads to disasters how bird died in the story. Take ways of story are: Jealousy is Suicidal; People living together should not quarrel among themselves. Unity is Strength. Differences of Opinions should be solved by proper discussion and negotiations

Snake, mongoose and Heron: is the best tale to explain the consequences of one's greed. When you are trying to kill your enemy in the business world may leads to ending their own business or work life. It also gives morale that 'Solution of the problem should not be worse than the problem itself'. Take away of story are Greed invites retributions, Solution of the problem should not be worse than the problem itself, Don't be the victim of foolish suggestions, No one gives you a free suggestions or consultation without own benefits.

Clever Rabbit, Proud Lion: is the best to teach the morale of Intelligence is superior to the physical strength. Always need to keep in mind that, one can't win the game by using only physical strength in game ground. It is very important understand that, intelligence helps to overcome worst situations of day to day business wit out any adverse effects. Take ways of the story are Intelligence is superior to the physical strength, Deceive the wicked and destroy them without mercy, One shouldn't be panic in the critical situations; one should be clever enough to think out of the box to solve the issues.

Timid Bramin's Crab friend: an opportunity to understand the need of troop or partners in the business. A Bramin's while travelling to another place, carried a crab along with him as per the suggestion of his mother.

During the journey, a Bramin was taking rest under the tree and a snake came by sensing the smell, but before even it harms him, crab had a fight with snake and killed it. So the story tells us that to be a one among team members. Take ways of the story are Never Embark the journey alone, always listen to the elders, Each and every one are helpful in various situations.

But life is not a path of flowers: When one believes in oneself, sheds bad companionship and sets realistic goals to achieve, success can be achieved. But Panchatantra warns that the path is not of flowers and one will face difficult situations. One should be prepared for evils and not panic, as taught in the story of 'The Monkey and the Crocodile' - that difficult situations require witty solutions, which get clouded when we panic or become emotional. Through the story of 'The Cunning Hare and the Witless Lion', the Panchatantra teaches us to constantly use intelligence and knowledge to overcome all evils that come in our path to success.

These simple lessons show us an easy path to success: A treatise of ancient India, Panchatantra packages the wisdom of ages for people of all classes. Through simple yet enchanting stories, it teaches us important lessons of life that we tend to overlook as we mature. This is despite of the fact that the wisdom it carries enlightens us with the path to success, and lead a life of peace. In this ever dynamic and competitive world, these lessons become more relevant in today's context than ever before!

Be yourself and more importantly believe in yourself: The Story of the Blue Jackal' teaches the importance of being oneself. We can fool others about our appearance, qualifications, possessions, knowledge - but that does not work in a long run and eventually we get caught. It is important of being confident, when being oneself. Only somebody who does not believe in oneself, retorts to cheap show-offs. It is thus important to believe in oneself, which is what 'The Brahmin and the Crooks' illustrates us. Belief works wonders in our struggle for accomplishments while we lose possessions, position and prestige when we fail to believe in ourselves.

Companionship matters not just in the early ages but throughout the life. Through the story of 'The Turtle That Fell off the Stick', the Panchatantra demonstrates us the importance of being with, and listening to advices of friends who are wise and wish us well. Issues that come of bad companionship is highlighted in 'Right-Mind and Wrong-Mind' and other stories, but the Panchatantra works on real world and redefines "bad company". We may have good and loyal friends, who are well-wishers but they may lack the intelligence or knowledge to accompany you to your path to accomplishments. Through the story of 'The King and the Foolish Monkey' we get the lesson that a foolish friend can do more harm than an enemy, and should be done away as bad company.

It is very important for one to have necessary skills to tackle the difficult challenges arises in the day to day activities and also to an effective utilisation of opportunities come to us. Teaching these skills in the formal education in the theoretical classes is the biggest challenge for teachers and professional trainers. Here is an opportunity for the Universities, Colleges and Companies to adopt these Panchtantra stories to teach required skills and morale in the easiest and effective manner. Significant efforts were made to analyse and understand the Panchtantra Tales and its applicability in the management education with the objectives of imparting the life skills and managerial skills among the youth as these are very much necessary in the present era. Study shows that, majority of the Panchtantra tales can be adopted in the syllabus in order to swallow required skills. As these tales are self-explanatory and it will be easy for students to understand the contents adopted and also can be inculcated among them. These skills will be very useful for them in the coming days as well as in the corporate world.

In summary, it can be said that Panchatantra has vital importance in the world literature for its contribution in the field of practical wisdom. In India, it was narrated to teach the students who were not much interested in studies. The disinterest of students about learning is a major problem of modern education where Panchatantra can come to help as a technique in bringing these students again towards schools and education. Panchatantra has an element of entertainment, wisdom, creativity and logical thinking. Use of all these elements can be useful to the teachers, students and parents. It might help the teachers to understand how to involve students in the process of learning and how to weave the threads of knowledge with the threads of entertainment. It also reflects about psychology, philosophy and general human tendencies. Panchatantra is a piece of ancient Indian literature which can be useful in the modern education because of its specialties (for example, frame story) and can still contribute a lot with a directed and dedicated research.

CHAPTER NINETEEN

Animal Kingdom Leadership Lessons

If you keep your eyes open and are willing to learn, life offers you invaluable advice at every step of the way. Very recently I realized the huge role that the Wild, especially the Animal Kingdom, plays in teaching us important management and leadership skills

Animals that travel in groups, when making migratory or movement decisions, often depend on social interactions among their own group members. This is done by signaling one another or making noises which can only be understood by their own species. The leader leads by example, takes responsibility of the safety of its followers and in turn the followers are dependent on their leader. Apart from good leadership, there are many qualities that we can imbibe from the Wild.

Working hard, like ants: Perhaps the most important trait if you want to succeed in any aspect of life is to work hard. There is a host of animals associated with hard work, but the one that stands out is of course the ant. Around 12,000 ant species have been discovered so far. These different species have more or less the same castle system. This system consists of queens at the top, then soldier ants, worker ants, and fertile males. Each class has a specific role to perform within the colony. The queen lays down eggs, and both soldier and worker ants perform a variety of tasks such as feeding the larvae, cleaning the eggs and foraging for food. Furthermore, one research found that we have a striking similarity to ants: we both value hard-earned rewards for our work. The research was quite simple. Ants were placed in front of two paths to get a specific reward. There was one easy path, where they just had to travel in a horizontal line, and another, much more complicated. Results showed that whatever the reward at the end of the path, ants always chose the hard path. This clearly demonstrates a willingness to work hard, and that hard-earned rewards just feel better, and in this case taste better.

Communicating and working in teams, like wolves: Wolves travel in packs. These packs have a hierarchical structure, with the alpha male and female as leaders of the pack, and predefined roles and responsibilities such as protecting the pack or hunting for the rest. Additionally, wolves use a combination of howling, snaps, and body language to communicate over close and long distances, to warn of threats and survive together. These techniques and situations apply to the workplace. Teams that stick together, know their respective roles and responsibilities and communicate effectively have a higher chance of tackling challenges and thriving in a competitive market.

Leading like lions: Ever since we were kids, we have been told and taught that the lion is the king of the jungle. Think of popular movies like The Lion King, children's books, and National Geographic documentaries. We can learn a lot about leadership from these animals, by closely examining their behavior individually or within their prides. For example, the traits that are often associated with lions, such as courage, strength, and decisiveness, are also the main traits that can make you stand out and be a great leader. Additionally, **lions are social animals** that live in groups of 10 to 15. These groups consist of lionesses, whose role is to hunt, cubs, and lions who are there to protect the pride.

Having a great vision, like eagles: Eagles have been objects of admiration and fascination throughout history. Just think of the number of countries with eagles in their flag or as their symbol, or sports teams with eagles as their name or mascot. It is probably a lot. This fascination is due to certain characteristics that make eagles unique. Great vision, fearlessness, great care of and affection for their eaglets, and their overall power make eagles a great example of leadership and success. Successful leaders are known to have a vision for their career or business, to take risks, to be fearless in order to grow, and to take care of their employees and colleagues.

Adapting to change, like chameleons: Being able to adapt to change is crucial. It ensures you can incorporate into new teams, initiate new partnerships, and generally be successful. We can learn how to adapt to certain situations by observing some species that reacted effectively to external factors, like wood frogs that freeze their bodies to survive the winter, or crocodiles, which have been around for 80 million years. However, when we think of change and camouflage, we often think of chameleons. Well, there is a misconception as to why chameleons change their colors. Scientists believe that chameleons change their skin color to reflect their mood or in reaction to the climate. For example, some chameleons tend to be dark in the winter to retain more heat and stay warm. Wouldn't it be great to show your mood to others without saying anything, or blending into new teams smoothly?

Having the right attitude, like elephants: Recruiters nowadays often look for candidates with the right attitude, personality, and soft skills, to ensure they will blend in easily and work effectively within teams. Elephants are prime examples of animals that demonstrate a great sense of empathy, calmness, togetherness, determination, and of course a great memory. Throughout history, elephants have been able to learn different moves and commands easily in order to perform at public shows or carry out specific daily tasks. Further evidence of elephants' intelligence is their proven ability to memorize and manipulate tools in their surroundings to get things done.

Renewal – Accept changes, learn and grow: When eagles are 30 years old, they go through a process of renewal. Finding a hidden place high in the mountains, the old eagle begins to claw and tears out the old feathers that by now become less airborne. As a result, it bleeds badly. But this is vital for the eagle in order to renew its strength. It is thus vital for the eagle to undergo this change to gain its strength and builds its resilience. Likewise, every manager should be open to change and embrace new ideas and technologies to integrate, grow and transform its businesses.

Develop Skillset like Leopard: The leopard is a highly agile animal that adjusts its efforts to suit its needs. Sometimes it relies on stealth, at other times speed, and at other times agility. For example, it can track its prey on the ground and also climb trees to hunt. It can move silently though the forest and at the same time marshal a burst of speed to close in. Lesson: Leaders and organizations that are adaptable can be assured greater opportunities to achieve success than those that rely on a more limited mindset and skillset

Constantly managing with the Changes to Show Flexibility: When it comes to flexibility or resilience, dictionaries usually mean the ability to quickly recover from difficult situations. In the animal world, there is only one animal that has never changed over the past one thousand years. What it was in the olden times is just like today. It is the crocodile. It can live both on land and water. Its power remains the same in both the situations while its revealed part of the body is covered with amour that prevents the hunters from its prey.

Preserve Inadequate Resources for Survival Mode: In this natural world, most animals have the habit of conserving their food for the winter so to hibernate since their movement is quite difficult in the severe weather and they wait for the perfect time when the winter comes to an end. Bear lives in colder regions and goes into hibernation for about six months. Same is the case with organisations. Businesses in difficult and recessionary period must conserve their resources and cut out their unnecessary expenses. These companies survive for a longer time and perhaps sustain than the ones that follow the approach of running the business as usual.

Leverage Your Core Competency With Respect To Speed: When talking about the core competency with respect to time, Cheetah is an animal that hunts for its prey in the earliest time with complete attention. Similarly, if businesses plan to focus on their core competency like on time shipment or excellent products or services, they can easily compete with the renowned competitors and become notable.

Versatility Feature: Pure versatility or adaptability is the feature that no animal possesses other than the dog. The dog is the animal that has the capability to live with the human beings. It has evolved its nature to live an easy life and ensuring survival. Similarly, people have the ability to adopt the environment and surroundings rapidly, without affecting their productivity. Organisations that are adaptable to such changes succeed than the ones who don't have the flexibility. We all know that animals adopt the changing environments and surroundings unconsciously or without any conscious effort. Though human beings and organisations are different, but they can adopt change if intended to do so.

Be like Turtle: From the moment a baby sea turtle leaves the confines of its nest, danger is ever present. While it may leave the nest with its siblings, much of its singular journey will be spent alone. Yet it is the endurance and the stamina required to stay alive that propels the turtle. They understand it is a marathon, not a sprint. Their undertaking takes place over a long distance and over a long period of time which demands great physical and mental stamina. Turtles, known for slow and steady progress, model endurance — take your time, think deeply, swim confidently through fast waters, learn from failure, and always find your way home. To improve your own endurance and stamina, schedule a standing meeting weekly with yourself. Use the time to reflect, read, write, strategize, take a walk, or practice mindfulness. Female sea turtles give their children the opportunity to emerge from a nest close to the water and let the moon and the sun guide their journey. Educators love and guide many, many students over the years sometimes even through what might be described as the lost years, or as I like to say the years where they are searching. We help students reach their full potential and find their individual talents and passions often after some trial and error. This should be the highest priority of education. Students, and teachers, need to exercise independent choice to find fulfillment, challenge, and happiness in their work. Heads must create and foster this culture of independence, curiosity, and creativity.

CHAPTER TWENTY

Lessons from the planting Seed

Growth is a rough and often painful process.

Seeds come in different shapes and sizes, with each type having different requirements for germination (the process in which seeds sprout and begin to grow). Small seeds must be placed as delicately as possible in the soil so that they do not get buried too deep. They should also be planted together in groups, ensuring that some will grow into thriving plants. Larger seeds, on the other hand, are buried deeper and generally with fewer in a group. Some seeds prefer warm, dry environments, while others require environments that are cold and moist. There are seeds that will germinate in less than five days, while others will take five months—or even longer.

Accepting this belief is essential to fulfilling your ambitions and goals. Looking at nature, we see that maturation is often a challenging process.

Once upon a time, there was a seed. A giant tree was once a tiny lifeless seed that underwent a massive transformation.

When the seed is planted in the soil, it slowly expands to the point where it can no longer bear its original form. To evolve to its next stage, it must split into pieces, completely shedding its former identity. If we observe only this stage, we see the seed destroyed.

However, in its new form, the former seed continues to grow and develop, becoming a gigantic tree with deep roots, strong branches, vibrant green leaves, blooming flowers, and nutritious fruit.

As leaders, we must ask the important questions during the rough times on our journey. What would happen if the seed were never planted? If it never underwent the transformation toward its full potential?

Like the seed, we must dare our comfort zone and dive into new experiences. Like the sun, we must be humble enough to embrace our strengths and imperfections. When we understand the "Law of the Seed", we don't get so disappointed when our efforts do not bear fruit. We stop feeling like victims. We remind ourselves that it is a law of nature, and we need to try again and harder. We learn how to deal with failure effectively.